A History of Women's Lives in Eastbourne

A History of
Women's Lives
in Eastbourne

Tina Brown

PEN & SWORD HISTORY

AN IMPRINT OF PEN & SWORD BOOKS LTD.
YORKSHIRE - PHILADELPHIA

First published in Great Britain in 2019 by
Pen & Sword History
An imprint of
Pen & Sword Books Ltd
Yorkshire – Philadelphia

ISBN 9781526716194

Printed and bound in England by TJ International, Padstow, Cornwall

Pen & Sword Books Limited incorporates the imprints of Atlas, Archaeology,
Aviation, Discovery, Family History, Fiction, History, Maritime, Military,
Military Classics, Politics, Select, Transport, True Crime, Air World,
Frontline Publishing, Leo Cooper, Remember When, Seaforth Publishing,
The Praetorian Press, Wharncliffe Local History, Wharncliffe Transport,
Wharncliffe True Crime and White Owl.

For a complete list of Pen & Sword titles please contact

PEN & SWORD BOOKS LIMITED
47 Church Street, Barnsley, South Yorkshire, S70 2AS, England
E-mail: enquiries@pen-and-sword.co.uk
Website: www.pen-and-sword.co.uk

Or
PEN AND SWORD BOOKS
1950 Lawrence Rd, Havertown, PA 19083, USA
E-mail: Uspen-and-sword@casematepublishers.com
Website: www.penandswordbooks.com

Contents

Introduction

So much of the focus of the suffrage and women's rights tends to centre around the larger towns and cities of England, however if you delve a bit deeper into the history, you will find yourself embarking on an incredible journey which will take you through time and change. When I first started researching Eastbourne I was quite disappointed at the distinct lack of historical content I could find and I almost gave up. However, I decided to take a different approach and was totally absorbed by the subject, tracing the lives of influential ladies who either were born, or spent time in or around the coastal town of Eastbourne during the period 1850 to 1950. As you read through the pages of this book you will see just how the lives of many British women changed so much, in so many ways, including Acts of Parliament being passed, which brought forth new changes in laws in education, work and divorce and marriage rights. There was no doubt that this was a significant time which would go on to shape history for future generations in so many ways.

Struggle and suffrage does not just cover the fights for rights and votes for women, although this was one significant chapter. The struggle so many of the women had to face was on a day to day basis in areas of work and home life and just trying to get their voices heard for the first time.

The Votes for Women campaign was one aspect of a gradual and slow-moving improvement in women's rights that had been an ongoing presence throughout the nineteenth century. The movement also campaigned for the right to divorce a husband, to have the right to education and the right to be able to work in the professions. Many women saw the vote as the catalyst that would give them a say in the laws of the country which affected their daily lives and had the potential for so much change. By the end of the period covered in this book, up and down the country, including in Eastbourne, the voices of women were starting to be heard and acted on.

The struggle and suffrage which many women faced touched every corner of the country, including the resort town of Eastbourne on the south-east coast. The women of this town, famous for being a garden resort by the sea, faced challenging times during both the First and Second World War, with many facing the day to day struggle of making ends meet.

In this book you will meet remarkable and incredible women, who have been linked or connected to the town of Eastbourne. Some were born in Eastbourne others moved there, but they all share the common bond of fighting for the rights and beliefs of women to make their voices heard not just locally, but up and down the country and to improve the lives and opportunities for women for future generations, not just from Eastbourne, but nationally.

Each chapter covers a different aspect of life for women in Eastbourne, from home life and work to educational opportunities and leisure pursuits. There will be a brief focus on any relevant laws which were implemented, with links to how the women of Eastbourne directly fought to change the lives of many women. You will read first-hand accounts from women of the area, and I am very grateful to them for sharing their life experiences with me for this publication. Sharing in the experiences of these women will open your mind to the difficulties they faced on a day to day basis and the dedication and perseverance they showed to their work. My research has brought the women of Eastbourne to life for me in so many ways; so many women, and their fascinating lives, have been introduced to me that I would never have known about. What strikes me as I have been writing this is how you find yourself identifying with them, cheering them on, laughing and crying with them, sharing the life they endured and in turn contributed so much to society.

CHAPTER ONE

Education and Professional Life

During the 100 years from 1850 to 1950, one area which saw significant change was education and professional training, not just for the middle and upper classes, for whom education and learning was available, but also for the working classes and the poor, thus opening educational opportunities to so many more people than before. During the 1860s, Parliament funded most schools and the annual bill for this exceeded £800,000, with growing pressures for more schools to be provided in areas where none had previously existed. Religion played a large part in how and where schools were run and there was huge debate as to whether the state should fund schools which had some religious interest, or whether schools should have no association with any denomination. Things were set to change and in 1869, the National Education League was formed, which began its campaign for free, compulsory and non-religious education for all children, regardless of class. There were also the concerns raised by the industrialists that provision of education was now vital for the country to lead Britain forward in manufacturing; a thought which was backed by much weight in Parliament. If Britain was to remain at the forefront of industry, then it needed to prepare for the future. This meant educating more of the population in subjects which would be of use to industry, business and the country as a whole. When the Education Act was passed in 1870, it was a monumental step as it was the first law which dealt with the provision of education in Britain.

It was an important turning point in how education was viewed as it demonstrated the commitment to providing education to all on a national scale. The Act allowed voluntary schools to continue to work as they had done, but it also set up a system of much needed school boards to build and manage the schools in the areas of the country where they were most needed. The school boards were elected locally and were funded by local rates. In these schools, the religious teaching was to be non-denominational, however, specific religious teaching continued in the voluntary schools. Even so, the issue of making education compulsory for all children, boys and girls, had not been settled by this Act and it took the Royal Commission on the Factory Acts in 1876 to recommend that education was to be made compulsory to try and eliminate child labour. In 1880, further changes were made to the Education Act which meant that attending school for education was mandatory for all children between the ages of 5 and 10. However, statistical records show that in the early 1890s attendance for children within this age group was only at 82 per cent; short of what the law had hoped to have achieved.

The implementation of the Elementary Education (Blind and Deaf Children) Act of 1893 established schools for children with special needs, which was closely followed in 1899 by the provision of the Elementary Education (Defective and Epileptic Children) Act, which focused on offering physically impaired children the same educational opportunities as able-bodied children. By the 1890s there were some 2,500 school boards throughout England and Wales which had been set up because of this new legislation. There were some concerns, however, voiced by the voluntary schools as to the lack of funding they received when compared with the financial assistance received by the other schools. It was in 1902 that a new Education Act was proposed by A.J. Balfour (who was to later become prime minister) aimed at greatly reorganising the administration of education at a local level. The school boards were scrapped throughout England and Wales and all elementary schools were placed in the hands of local education authorities, which were directly under the control of the county borough councils. It was under this Act that significant provision was made for secondary and technical education and councils were encouraged to subsidise grammar schools and provide free places for children from working-class families. The growth of secondary education for all was slow to take off, with its primary focus still being on the middle classes.

It was not just the education of the children which Parliament wanted to change, but also that there had to be changes to ensure that children were healthier. In 1906, poor schoolchildren received help under the Education (Provision of Meals) Act. This enabled councils to be able to provide meals which were free of charge when parents could not afford to pay for them, which was later made compulsory by the Education Act in 1944. The health and welfare of the children was of such concern that in 1907 the Education Act required education authorities to ensure that all children under their care received medical inspection.

By 1914, Britain had a basic education system in place, although for the majority, this did not extend beyond the age of 12 years old. The First World War brought about new concerns and it was H.A. Fisher, the president of the board of education, who raised the issues he had observed as he travelled around Britain inspecting schools, after becoming critically aware of the problem faced schools by underfunding. Fisher was forward thinking in his ideas and was fundamental in the Education Act of 1918, which aimed to make vast improvements in the availability of education and to make significant changes in education. He believed it was not only vital for everyone, but also for society and he fought to make his voice heard. Changes were made which included increasing the leaving age from 12 to 14 years and introducing further education classes for those in work from the age of 14 to 18. The Act also saw much improved education for nursery schools and special needs education. There were also improvements to funding and the responsibility passed from local councils to central government, which in turn created a greater sense of professionalism amongst the teachers by increasing salaries and pensions for the first time. These were slow to be implemented due to the economic downturn of the 1920s which continued to grip Britain until well after the end of the Second World War.

Following the end of the Second World War, secondary education was set to change by vast improvements being made to remove the inequalities which were very present in the education system. More free places at grammar schools were made available, however these were often turned down by the poorer families due the additional costs involved in their child receiving their education at such an establishment. It was not until the Education Act of 1944 that free secondary education was provided for all pupils. Another change which was brought in was the introduction of the 11-plus examination, a system which would allow children to be allocated education on the results of this exam. The 11-plus was intended to provide equal education for all, regardless of sex or background. Subsequent years saw the school leaving age eventually being raised to 16 in 1972. For the first time both sexes were being recognised in the realms of education and doors were opening for women.

Eastbourne had several women who were instrumental in making changes for women in education, both as learners and teachers.

Emily Phipps (1865–1943): Emily was an important figure in the National Union of Teachers and strived and achieved so much as well as being a headmistress, a feminist and a barrister. On her death in 1943, one obituary said of her 'There seems to be nothing she could not do if she turned her attention to it'. Sadly today, Emily seems to have been forgotten, and this once strong and witty lady, who was the inspiration to so many female teachers needs her story to be heard.

She was the oldest of five children and was born on 7 November 1865 in Devonport. Her parents were Henry John Phipps and Many Ann Frost. Emily's father worked at Devonport Dockyard. She spent her life being totally committed to feminism and together with her friend Clara Neal became a member of the Women's Freedom League in 1908 following an anti-suffrage meeting in Swansea, and as a result they set up their own local branch. Emily was also passionate about injustice to animals and humans, which she campaigned tirelessly for.

Emily was known for setting up a protest on the night of the 1911 census, by staying overnight in a cave on the Gower coastline. She tirelessly campaigned for most of her life until 1925 when she retired from her head mistress's post in London due to ill health, and moved to share a house with Adelaide Jones, a former teacher and good friend. In 1939 they were living in Eastbourne at 26 Arundel Road, where they lived happily for many years, until Emily passed away from a heart condition in 1943.

During her working life, Emily was an active member for the National Union of Women Teachers (NUWT), which was formed in 1906 as part of the National Union of Teachers (NUT). From 1915, Emily served as president for three years and in 1917 was the editor of the NUWT Journal. She made sure that this journal was forward thinking and focused, unlike many of the journals available at the time for women teachers, which primarily wrote about fashion and recipes.

Whilst working as a teacher, Emily studied for the bar in her spare time and was admitted as a barrister in 1925, which was when she gave up teaching.

She lived by a wonderful saying: 'If you make yourself a doormat, do not be surprised if people tread on you'.

A remarkable lady!

The *Dundee Telegraph* of 1887 reported on the higher education of women:

> *The effort for higher education is simply an effort to secure in the case of women what has always been the case with men. Women's ideals should be formed, as men's have been, by those who have lived out of the roar of traffic, out of the glare of politics, far from the influence of mobs, away from the contamination of commerce and drudgery of manual labour. The women we want to form women's ideal of education are women with calm well-balanced minds and hallowed hearts, equal to men in ideas and mental*

prowess, if inferior to them in physical endurance, and perhaps making up in spiritual insight for their lack of physical strength. This is the goal towards which we invite all women to strive whose position is fortunate enough to enable them to do so.

This interesting article seems to suggest that women could be educated only if they were of the right sort of disposition, as men did not want women to use their education to make gains on their male counterparts!

Eastbourne was a popular place to send middle- and upper-class young women, especially those from the northern industrial towns and cities of England, to gain a good and solid education. Many new schools were established in the town in the late 1800s to accommodate the influx of students, including ones such as St Mary's Girls' School, which in 1895, placed an advertisement for two educated young women to assist teaching the younger girls, explaining that 'Interested parties should apply to the Head Mistress'. This would have been a common form of advertisement and was relatively cheap to place in a newspaper or periodical of the time.

It was common place for well-educated and upper-class girls to be sent away to school to another town and Eastbourne, on the south coast, was one such option as it appealed to many parents looking for a suitable education and environment for their daughters. Greencroft Girls' School, which offered all examinations and quiet and extensive grounds for leisure pursuits, was advertised in the *Sheffield Daily Telegraph*, in 1926.

In January 1927, *The Scotsman* ran an advertisement for Fairfield Court Girls' School, in Eastbourne. The school was described as offering a thorough education and options to study at graduate and masters level, not to mention individual attention, sports facilities, and a large spacious house and grounds.

The young ladies who were educated at Eastbourne's private schools often went on to great things and *The Eastbourne Gazette* of 1937 reported on former Eastbourne girls who were now school teachers working as missionaries in Palestine. Miss

Cane from the United Missionary Service League spoke at a meeting at the All Souls' Church Room and described in detail the work of the young women connected with the missionary. She spoke of the great difficulties that the young women often encountered in their work; one of the biggest problems being many Jews, who were not religious. She also talked about the value of the missionary schools both academically and from the point of view of Christianity, 'The schools are marvellous proof of power of Christ in a hostile world'. She explained that there was still urgent need for more missionary work, especially from a medical point of view.

In the late 1930s, things were changing for higher education for women and a public notice was advertised in the *Eastbourne Herald* in 1939 on behalf of the Eastbourne Higher Education Committee, stating that the School of Arts and Crafts would be offering an evening class and any interested people should send their names to the school secretary immediately. The introduction of this type of education in the form of evening classes meant that more women could attend, rather than the usual day time courses which were held when they were at work. Many women welcomed this alternative teaching style and were grateful for the freedom and independence education brought with it, which in the past had only been available to the privileged few.

By 1949, education had gone through numerous changes and in that year the Eastbourne Technical College ran an advert for an experienced hairdresser (male or female) to teach practical hairdressing two afternoons a week. It stated that the position would suit someone who was either a married lady or a retired gentleman. This showed how the subjects taught had changed from the 1800s to the mid-1900s, from the more traditional to the vocational subjects.

Rosalie Harvey – Medical Missionary Worker

Many women in the late 1800s wanted so much more than the life they were expected to lead, which consisted of marrying a suitable gentleman, often selected by parents of the middle or upper classes, and so women often looked at alternatives, such as taking up positions abroad, or providing humanitarian work. One such lady from Eastbourne who followed this path was Rosalie Harvey. She spent a great deal of her life in India where, for over fifty years, she dedicated her time to looking after neglected animals and people. Rosalie, the daughter of a vicar, was born in the 1850s in the town of Seaford, a short distance to the west of Eastbourne. From a very early age Rosalie dreamed of helping animals and people who were less fortunate than herself, and this, combined with the stories she learned about the Far East, captured her imagination. When she was 28 years old she went to Poona, India with the Zenana Medical Mission, and a short time later moved on to Nasik, where she worked for the rest of her life. Not on any occasion could Rosalie be persuaded to leave her work and take a short break to visit her family.

Miss Harvey's fifty-year dedication really made a mark on the people of Poona and they loved her. The sick and wounded animals and people she helped numbered over 1,500, many of whom were young babies and children. One of the children she helped nursed Rosalie through her last illness, looking after her and taking care of her as she had done to so many.

When Rosalie looked back on her time, she knew that her work with the lepers was her greatest achievement. During years of plague and famine she had worked in a relief camp and met such terrible cases of leprosy that she felt nothing mattered except caring for these people. She begged a little money, built an iron shelter for thirty-five lepers and remained in charge until the end.

The people of Poona called her 'Ayai', the mother. There were those to whom she was the light in heaven. At one point she was given the Kaisar-i-Hind gold medal in honour of her work. However, she always said that she did not need any medals, just the homes and care she gave her people and animals. When she became unwell and sadly passed away, all she asked was that her work would continue after her.

Another remarkable lady who studied in the area was Peggy Angus.

Peggy Angus

Peggy came from a large family and spent much of her childhood in Chile, however she maintained her Scottish roots and on returning from Chile she was sent away to be educated in Scotland. She spent a period studying at the Eastbourne School of Art, which opened her career as a well-known artist and designer, specialising in industrial art and wallpaper designs.

She rented a house known by the name of Furlongs, in Eastbourne and lived there in 1933. Her house became a hive of activity for many of her contemporaries and she often met with Eric Ravilious, another designer. Her home was important to her and she was always looking for new ways to improve its homely feel and atmosphere. She would ask friends to assist her in her home improvements even though she was a capable artist, with an incredible eye for detail. Furlongs was described by many as a completely magical place and ever so welcoming from the moment you first stepped through the front door. Peggy was known for her endless enthusiasm and vision and despite her ill health she was determined to keep going. She passed away in 1998 at the age of 88, after a long and fulfilling life.

CHAPTER TWO

Working Life

Home working, professionals, changes in work during the First and Second World War.

Life of the female smuggler in Eastbourne

One of the first documented occupations of poorer women in the Eastbourne area is connected with the rich smuggling history in this part of the country. Along the Sussex coast and around Eastbourne there was an area which was frequented by this trade called Beachy Head; a rocky headland known for its treacherous coastline, where ships would often run aground.

It was said that many local women were involved in smuggling as the illicit trade grew. Male smugglers involved their families and girlfriends with the presumed idea that their activities would be less easy to detect if they were being carried out by a female than a male. Women were reported to have tied lace and tea into their clothing, especially into the sleeves and hemlines of dresses, which could easily disguise these smuggled goods. Some women were reported to have carried so much contraband that they had to conceal the goods around their abdomen, making them look as if they were pregnant. Smuggling was highly prosperous and a great deal of money was made at a time when obtaining goods in the normal way involved paying huge taxes, and so the general population had little choice other than to turn to smuggling to get hold of such items. There were, of course, fatalities connected with the smuggling trade and one local girl,

Elizabeth Collins, who was known as Peg, lost her life to the contraband (or blockade) guards who patrolled the Beachy Head area. She was said to be the daughter of a blacksmith who owned a farm over the Downs. Peg took to smuggling as she was very quick and was more of a tomboy than a young lady. She helped her father on the farm and assisted her uncle with fishing. Going out off the coast in the boat on a regular basis meant that it wasn't long before Peg became involved in bringing contraband goods, disguised as fish and sea foods, ashore.

However, one unfortunate night, Peg and her uncle were mistaken as two notorious smugglers and were shot by the contraband guards. It wasn't until their boat was searched and only fish found that they realised that on this occasion they had been incorrect in their judgement. Sussex smugglers were said to be the most desperate, and were known for their notorious and often violent deeds, which often included cruel and barbarous murders.

Looking forward into the Victorian period and beyond

Work for women was very limited and depending on your class, if a woman wanted to work this could be viewed very differently. For example, for middle-class and upper-class women to even consider working or employment in any way was frowned upon during the Victorian years. It was considered to be the role of the husband to provide and support his wife, so that she had no need to seek employment and could stay at home and do what wealthy Victorian women did. No thought was given to the fact that life for these women was incredibly boring, with little to do, and even their friends and acquaintances were selected and visits outside of the house would often be chaperoned – why should a woman want or need to leave her home without her husband? If a woman was seen out on her own it was looked on as a negative event and that she must be doing something she shouldn't be, or maybe conducting an illicit affair. As many of these relationships were completely devoid of any warmth or affection, some women did seek this outside of their marriage, bearing in mind that their husband also did – but for them this behaviour was accepted. It wasn't until much later and the start of the First World War that things started to change.

The impact of the First World War on the world was huge and it was felt everywhere by everyone. Everyone had a member of their family who was fighting, or knew someone who was caught up in the terribleness of it all. Eastbourne itself did not suffer as much in the First World War as it was to in the Second World War. People of the town remember the time when the workhouse was cleared to make way for an army hospital, and the sound of bands accompanying the dead as their coffins made their way to Ocklynge Cemetery. The sound could be heard all over the town. Another sad reminder of all the lives lost during the war years was when HMS *Hampshire was* sunk off Marwick Head, Orkney, on 5 June 1916, with only twelve survivors. The bodies of more than 700 men were washed up on the shore and although most of them were unrecognisable, Lieutenant Colonel Oswald Arthur Gerald Fitzgerald, Kitchener's military secretary, was identified and brought back to Eastbourne and buried at Ocklynge Cemetery, after a funeral at All Saints Church. On the day of the funeral procession, nearly everyone in Eastbourne turned out to pay their respects and lined the streets to bid farewell. His coffin had been in state in St Matthews Church, Westminster, before its journey to Victoria Station and then on to Eastbourne. When it arrived, it was transferred to a gun carriage drawn by six horses as it made its way to All Saints Church.

Eastbourne itself was involved in helping many of the families and people who had been directly affected by the activities of war and during this period, several local people extended the hand of friendship and love to those in need, be it wounded service men or refugees. Kindness was shown by strangers who offered lodgings in their own homes to people with no possessions or family around to support them.

Ms Christine Reid shared a story with me about her paternal grandmother, Mrs Naomi Miles, who ran a small gardening shop called 'Miller's Seed Store' on Seaside Road with her husband, Ernest. Sadly, Ernest was sent away to serve in the First World War in 1917, leaving Naomi alone to take care of the shop and business. Many women would have closed the shop and waited for their husband to return from the war, however, Naomi decided that she had to keep the shop open and running while her husband was away, so that it would still be there when he returned.

Naomi quickly decided that she could not keep the house, the shop and look after her small child, all on her own and so she made the decision to close her house in Birling Street in the Old Town of Eastbourne and move in with her in-laws, who lived just around the corner in Green Street. Her mother-in-law looked after the young child while Naomi rode her bicycle to and from the shop each day. At home in the evening, Naomi also had the ordering and the accounts to keep in good order, as well as looking after her young son. Ernest came home in 1919 to a business which was thriving and had been kept running by his efficient and business-savvy wife. Upon her husband's return Naomi returned to be a housewife and looking after the family home as she had done before. However, Naomi was a much stronger person than she had been before the war and had learnt a lot during her husband's absence.

The Women's Land Army (WLA) also played a huge role in the lives of Eastbourne and its women. Due to the numbers of men who had joined up during the First World War, farming and agriculture was at risk of total collapse. This, combined with supply boats being attacked in the channel, meant that Britain was on the brink of starvation – and so this is when the Women's Land Army stepped in. At the time, Britain relied heavily on the imports from its Empire, as it was only able to produce 35 per cent of its own food and so the plans were put in place to involve women in the growing and production of crops. What's more, in 1917 Britain saw a disastrous harvest and it was at this point that the Board of Agriculture created the Women's Land Army; a group of dedicated women whose role it was to take over the important duties within the farming and agricultural worlds.

Training positions were offered to women free of charge in the areas of milking, hop picking and fruit growing. For their work the women were paid 25 shillings a week, less 17 shillings for board and lodgings on the farms so that they were on hand to work all the time. East Sussex also had its own Women's Forestry Corps who worked closely alongside the WLA. Khaki-clad women were seen felling trees in the wooded areas around Eastbourne and Heathfield and were also sent to the Kent towns to work in the forests bordering Tunbridge Wells.

Sadly the WLA disbanded in 1919, but their huge efforts will always be recognised and remembered. Strong bonds and friendships were forged during these years between the women, many of whom stayed friends for the rest of their lives. These events would change the lives of many of the women in so many ways. The men were now returning from battle in Europe and this meant that the women who had worked in their roles were either released from their contracts or fired so that the men could once again take up their work.

Another example of women's roles in Eastbourne during the First World War was that of the female wartime staff at Eastbourne Post Office, who took over the roles of delivering the post in 1917. There was also mention of an Eastbourne lady by the name of Margaret Smith who became a taxi driver. Although originally born in France in 1882, she moved to Eastbourne when she was in her early twenties to run a boarding house; a role deemed as suitable for a woman to do. In 1916, Margaret obtained a driving licence and bought a motorcar. She enjoyed driving around and on some occasions people hired her to take them to special occasions. With the lack of men to take up roles as drivers, more women were allowed to drive taxis.

The First World War and Summerdown Camp in Eastbourne

A remarkable convalescent camp was set up on the edge of the town, known as Summerdown Camp. This camp was created to relieve the pressure on the town's military hospitals and further afield at the Queen Victoria Hospital (QVH) in East Grinstead, West Sussex, which was founded in 1863. QVH later went on to be world renowned for plastic surgery, as it is today. There were also civilian hospitals in Eastbourne and large houses (such as 9 Upperton Road and Fairfield Court) which were converted for military use to try and cope with the enormous number of casualties being brought to the camp. Often asylums were used and the patients were sent home to families who were not prepared, or even knew how, to look after their ill family member.

Summerdown was the first, and one of the largest convalescent camps. Its full title was the Summerdown Military Convalescent Hospital and it started off as a Royal Army Medical Corps Camp.

To help organise and assist with the number of casualties, a welcome hut was set up so that when men first arrived they would be met by lady volunteers and given refreshments, hot coffee and cake, and they were also able to talk to the volunteers who made the men feel at home. The soldiers really appreciated the kindness they were shown, even if it was from women who had little or no medical experience. Some of the women were friends of the camp organisers who had travelled from London to help out especially.

When the camp was complete it had a massage institute, dental clinic, shooting gallery, chapel, kitchens etc., it really was like a self-contained small town. There were craft shops such as basket making and carpentry all set up to help rehabilitate the men.

Romance did blossom at the camp; Private Joseph Pow of the 7th Battalion Royal North Lancashire Regiment was injured in France. During his convalescence in Summerdown Camp he met Frances Pullen who was working as a maid at a local girls' school. They were married in December 1917 and eventually went on to have eleven children.

The families of the convalescent soldiers were encouraged to visit Summerdown Camp to help with the men's well-being and rehabilitation. However, this was often costly, considering the travel and accommodation involved. The camp was unable to help with free accommodation but local people came to their aid. One such lady who was instrumental in arranging this was a Miss Alston, who lived on Summerdown Road. She saw the need for cheap accommodation for the visiting families and in 1915 set up the Empire Hostel at 51 Upperton Gardens, which offered cheap rates for rooms for the families. The hostel was so popular that it had to extend to the house next door and when it eventually closed in 1919 it had accommodated 1,500 guests.

Many families were unable to visit and so the local residents filled this gap by inviting the convalescent soldiers into their families and making them feel at home, organising parties etc.

Another lady whose actions helped the convalescent soldiers immensely was Mrs Pauline Almeric Paget, a wealthy American heiress who was married to an English MP. Sir Alfred Keogh, Director of Army Medical Services, was looking for qualified physiotherapists to be able to offer a fully comprehensive rehabilitation service plus remedial exercise and massage. However, suitably qualified people were in short supply. So, Sir Keogh turned to Mrs Paget who, in a very short space of time, was able to recruit some fifty certified masseuses who worked from the Pagets' London home – they became known as the Massage Corps. This was very successful and several others were soon set up across the country. Many of the women from the Almeric Paget Massage Corps worked at Summerdown and were identifiable from women in the nursing service by their simple uniform, with the badge of the APMC worn on the left arm, while those with red bars on the shoulders were worn by senior women.

The Massage Corps carried out a full range of treatments, including bathing, massage and special exercises. They also changed dressings, which was of high importance at the time, before the discovery of penicillin, and the risk of septic wounds becoming contaminated and hindering recovery times was high.

At Summerdown Camp, Mrs Paget also bought musical instruments for the band, a bell for the chapel, and at Christmas 1915 she paid for the soldiers to go to a pantomime in Brighton. You can see why this very special lady earned the name of the 'Angel of Summerdown'. Sadly, Mrs Paget passed away following a heart attack in November 1916 at the age of just 41 after suffering from chronic ill health.

Another lady who helped the soldiers was Lady Londonderry. She set up the Women's Legion in 1914 to promote a national volunteer movement for women who wanted to serve in the army. Initially, the Legion took on the roles of gardeners, cooks and waitresses, however, these roles expanded to include motor transport drivers in 1917. The cookery section was adopted in 1915 and this was so successful that it was taken up in other camps. Mrs Florence Burleigh Leach was put in charge of the cookery section and later became the head of the entire Women's Legion Cookery Section.

Another local lady who contributed to the care and well-being of the soldiers at Summerdown Camp was Miss Winifred Pattison. She made regular contributions to the camp journal on matters for camp gardening and encouraged the soldiers in gardening tuition.

Mrs Florence Burleigh Leach (later Dame Florence Simpson), the wife of a politician, took on the role of head of the cookery section at the camp, with the kitchens being staffed by the Women's Legion – a national volunteer movement for women who wanted to serve in the army. These women took on the roles of cooks, waitresses and gardeners at the camp and in 1917 the legion was renamed the WAAC, resulting in more women joining and being paid a wage.

So many lives were changed because of the kindness and generosity of the ladies mentioned above. Without them it would have been a very different situation for the soldiers trying to rehabilitate themselves and get over the harsh and appalling experiences they had had to endure.

The idea of Summerdown Camp was to treat thousands of injured soldiers and by the end of the war the camp had treated some 150,000 men. During its time it became a well-known and dominant feature of the town. Today the site of the camp is marked by 'Old Camp Road' at the junction of Pashley Road and Paradise Drive.

The Second World War and Changes in Work

Eastbourne suffered more air raid attacks than any other town in the south-east region – a total of 96. There were 174 fatalities and hundreds more injuries, 474 houses were destroyed and 10,000 more damaged. There were also 3 enemy aircraft shot down over the town and 200 people killed with 506 severely injured. On 11 September 1940, there was a general evacuation of the town of Eastbourne due to the threat of a German invasion. The first bombs fells on 7 July with the Technical Institute being damaged by the bombing.

The horrors of the war were felt on both sides – by the men and women actively serving and the families left at home. Mrs G. R. Ridley shared the following story with me about her mother's life during the Second World War:

World War II was a disaster for my mother. She was married in 1936 and gave birth to my two brothers, one in 1936 and then in 1938. My Dad was called up in 1940 and it was then that her world fell apart. Living in a tiny little flat, left on her own with very little income to support her two babies and feeling alone and frightened, Mum would often sleep in the Morrison shelter in the kitchen with my brothers. Possibly the happiest times were when she was drafted to work in a factory making aircraft landing mats and other items of machinery. The babies were looked after by the older ladies in the area and Mum would walk miles to and from work with some other ladies – this gave her some female company. Occasionally Dad would visit home as he was posted in the UK until 1943, before he was sent overseas until 1946.

Rationing became tougher, [Mum had] *very little money but her little boys kept her going. [Despite] resisting sending her eldest son to be an evacuee, her mind was changed when he was nearly killed. He had run around to the shop very close by for her (everyone knew all the children), ... he loved to be her big boy and help her as much as he could.*

A German plane swooped low and drifted down the road. The lady serving him grabbed him and somehow lifted him over the shop counter and sheltered him under the counter. He remembers all the tins and bottles crashing off the shelves. When the 'all clear' was given my terrified mother came running – the only time ever we think she ran in her life! He was then evacuated to the country.

So now [it was] just Mum and her youngest son with 'the beastly war' dragging on. Her husband was in the thick of fighting in North Africa and Italy and hopefully was still alive.

During 1944 there was a very bleak and bitter winter. A little life came back to the area in the shape of Canadian soldiers, residents opened their homes to them. This for Mum was a catastrophe – she became pregnant (with me) and I was born at the end of 1944. One can only imagine her despair and how tongues must have wagged. Her husband (away since January 1943) was called before his commanding officer abroad and given the news that his wife had had a child. He was asked to sign a paper to say that he would accept the child so that there would be money for Mum and me and that I could take his name. This must have been such a terrible shock for him.

My oldest brother remembers coming back from the country, Mum meeting him at the station with his brother and me – a strange little girl in a pram. As the war ended, Mum was determined to find a house for us all to live in, she walked the streets of Eastbourne and sat in the council offices until she was re-homed. By 1946, we were all in a three-bed house in Eastbourne.

This amazing man was the best dad to me. I did not know he was not my blood father until I was 22 and married. I will never know my blood father. I never asked and it was never, ever talked about. They were married for nearly sixty years. Mum and Dad had a further child in the 1950s, a sister for me. They all know about me but we are all very close, and after all it is our family history. Mum never talked about the war, only to say the following two sentences:

1. *Wars are evil and ruin lives.*

2. *Nobody knows or understand what the women left at home had to go through.*

Every Remembrance Day I put a wooden cross on Dad's grave with For My Hero written on it. I am not sure of the actual numbers of babies born in similar circumstances to me in the war. I guess it runs into thousands, I was lucky, I can only imagine others may not have been.

Some 48,000 Canadian servicemen married overseas during the Second World War with many couples meeting in the various dance halls and pubs in the cities and towns. For many women whose boyfriends and husbands were away, they were incredibly lonely and were grateful for the attention which was shown towards them by these foreign gentleman who arrived in their towns. Many married after only knowing each other for a brief amount of time. Indeed, there is one report of a marriage between a Canadian serviceman and an English woman taking place only forty-three days after the first Canadian soldiers arrived in England in November 1939.

However, not all relationships ended in marriage, and unfortunately some of the women became pregnant out of wedlock. This was a challenging time for anyone who was pregnant, let alone if you were unmarried. Single pregnant women were vulnerable and would be sent to live with strangers in the country so that they would be safe from any hostile wartime environment, while others were outcast by their families for being in their condition. For many of these young women, being sent to the country with no contact from anyone that they knew and no access to family and friends was an extreme ordeal for them to endure. Also, being in the countryside meant there was little if any access to any medical help or medications.

Dedicated Workers

In the old town area of Eastbourne, you will find the Parish Church of St Mary's with many interesting details and architectural features about it. The church had its own cleaner for some sixty years, a Mary Hart. Ms Hart passed away in the 1940s after her long and loyal service. Today you will find a tablet dedicated to her in St Mary's church. A reminder that even positions which were mainly domestic in nature were highly regarded by the worker and were lifelong occupations, showing a great deal of loyalty. This church also has a memorial window to two women who died within a few weeks of one another and this window was put up in memory of many blessings.

Businesses carried on as well as they could during the air raids and other activities of the war and one hairdresser's on Grove Road, Eastbourne, was no exception and they placed a small advertisement in the *Eastbourne Herald* on November 1940 to thank its customers:

> *Whittaker's, Ladies' and Gentleman's Hairdressers are still functioning in all branches. They are enabled to do so through the co-operation and loyalty of their more tenacious clients. They thank them. Also, that they still carry on during Air Raid Alerts.*

War impacted on and affected the lives of so many and not forgetting those who were left at home to carry on with life the best they could. Many women from Eastbourne signed up for the Land Army and the following is an article published in the *Eastbourne Herald*, 1944:

Land Army Talk

One of those pleasant afternoons which the Congregational Women's Own and Baptist Women's Fellowship spend together was enhanced on Wednesday by a visit from Mrs Dunlop, Women's Land Army (W.L.A.) representative. This lady, as you all know, was a member of the W.L.A. in the last war, and in this talk she drew an interesting comparison between the conditions which prevailed then and those which exist for land girls to-day. Everything has been much improved including wages, work, billets and equipment, and Eastbourne should be proud of the contribution the town has made to this invaluable service and never should the remark be passed "I did not know you had land girls in Eastbourne."

I think this article is very poignant as to how the women of Eastbourne felt about the war and how they wanted to contribute to the war effort in any way that they could.

During times of conflict and war, individuals can do incredible acts of kindness and one such person was a young girl who travelled to Eastbourne on holiday from Switzerland just before the Second World War broke out. The following is an article from the *Eastbourne Herald* in 1939:

Girl becomes Street Musician for Evacuees

A jolly auburn-haired girl, who came to Eastbourne from Switzerland on holiday and stayed here when war broke out is performing a piece of national service with a piano accordion. She has a simple message to you and I which is "please help the evacuees". The young lady's name is a Miss June Enstone who believes that her music can help the situation the world finds itself in now. June started helping by joining the Women's Voluntary Service and since then has been helping in numerous ways. She explained that one day it occurred to her that she might be able to raise funds to buy clothes for the poorer evacuees by playing her accordion in the streets of Eastbourne. She explained that when she approached the police about her idea they were very kind and supporting, all they asked of her was that she kept off the main shopping streets, which she agreed to and set up her pitch in the Meads and Upperton areas of the town. June's stepfather taught her how to play the accordion and she believes that she could not have had a better teacher. She said that she enjoys playing, however now she can put her accordion and her music to some use in helping other people at their time of need. Not only has June been playing

*to raise funds but she has also been entertaining soldiers at
a canteen and this was greatly received.*

The following article was written in the *Eastbourne Herald*
in 1941:

*'When that time comes, if men are still behind the lines, doing
women's work much against their will, while the men at the
front say in their thoughts: "Is there no end to this enemy?"
is a woman ever going to be able to look anybody in the face
again?' asked the Public Relations Officer for London and
the South-East, (Mr W. E. Oakley-Evans), at the inaugural
luncheon of the Eastbourne, Hastings and Bexhill War Work
Week, which was held at the Gildredge Hotel on Wednesday.*

*'The great need for women for the Forces (particularly the
ATB) and for munitions, and for older women to come
forward to take the place of the younger mobile women was
stressed urgently at the luncheon and the time had come for
sacrifice', said Mr H. B. Banner (Regional Information
Officer). 'No matter what sacrifice we made now it would
be well worth while', he added.*

*The lunch was well attended and guests included the Mayor
and men and women who knew how vital to the war effort
the woman power is today. The most stirring appeal of all
came from an ATS girl herself, Subaltern Denise Maxwell
Woosnam (Zone Recruiting Officer), who has been in the
service since the outbreak of war. She was among those ATS
girls who looked after gun sites north and south of the Thames
Estuary during last autumn's raids, and like the others stuck
to her post magnificently despite the falling bombs. Her
fiancé, an airman, was killed in the blitz last autumn.*

The *Eastbourne Herald* carried an interesting small snippet of
news on 13 September 1941:

*A young girl trainee from Eastbourne has been learning
munition work for the last four weeks. Everyone with
whom she has worked was very happy with the work and
her conduct, especially has she had such an eye for detail.*

Angela Olive Carter – Writer and Journalist (1940–1991)

Angela Olive Carter (later Pearce) who published as Angela Carter, was an English novelist, short story writer and journalist, known for her expressive feminist work. She was described as one of the boldest female writers of the twentieth century. Angela was born in Eastbourne in 1940 at the maternity home at 12 Hyde Gardens and passed away at her London home at the age of 51. Shortly after her birth, British forces started their retreat from Dunkirk meaning that the south coast of England became the front line of the war. Angela was evacuated to live with her maternal grandmother in South Yorkshire to spend the war years there, away from the dangers of Eastbourne and London.

Her first writing position was as a reporter for the Croydon Advertiser – following in her father's footsteps. One of her novels *Nights at the Circus* makes mention of her home town of Eastbourne and the fact that her mother was sent to Eastbourne during the Blitz.

Her father was a journalist and it was he who gave Angela the inspiration to pursue a much-loved career in writing. Although a feminist, Angela never set out to have her stories viewed and studied for their feminist messages. She would always stand up for women and their rights in the work place, even when her close male colleagues were given awards with little mention of females in their profession.

Mabel Lucie Attwell – Illustrator and Designer (1879–1964)

Mabel Lucie Attwell was born in 1879, and became a British illustrator known and loved for her nostalgic drawings of children, which were based on her own daughter. She lived during the 1930s at Ocklynge Manor in Mill Road, Eastbourne where a blue plaque commemorates her work and life. She illustrated many famous works including, *The Water Babies*, *Grimm's Fairy Tales* and *Alice In Wonderland*.

Mabel was a highly respected illustrator and designer and used the funny side of children and toddlers to inspire much of her work. During the First World War her husband, Harold, lost his right arm due to a shell explosion. Being right-handed he had to teach himself to draw again using his left hand. Following this accident Mabel became the breadwinner for the household and in 1918, J.M. Barrie asked her to illustrate his new book *Peter Pan*. During the 1940s and '50s Mabel designed dolls which were packaged in boxes illustrated with the beautiful designs. Her work is still hugely popular, as it was when she first began, ensuring that her name is still alive today. She used many of her observations from life around her for her illustrations; her own children and her friends' children were often models for her.

The 1940s were a dark time with many homes in Eastbourne and around the country having to use blackout curtains at night and constantly living in fear of attacks and air raids from the enemy. Air raid shelters were a normal part of life and one lady shared her own story about what she could remember as a small child spending time in them around Christmas time:

Mrs Eileen Donnell, Wolverhampton

I was born in 1933 and grew up in Eastbourne. I was one of eleven children and at the best of times things were hard for my Mum and Dad, let alone during the war. However, we never starved and somehow there was always food for us all. It must have been a great strain for Mum trying to provide for such a large family. I was the second youngest in the family with my older brothers and sisters quite a lot older than me and more like parents than siblings. They were often given the job of looking after me and my younger brother, especially when we had to go down the air raid shelter along the street. Often Mum would refuse to leave the house and would stay there [while] us lot always went along. She was always ok though as we were lucky that our house was never bombed, sometimes I would stay with Mum and we would hide together in the cupboard under the stairs, holding each other tight when we heard any loud noises nearby.

I used to hate the blackout curtains in the rooms; they made everything so very dark – sometimes me and one of my brothers would take a sneaky peek out through them into the street, just to see what was going on and we would always hear Mum shriek at us to close those curtains! We were glad when at the end of war, we could take down the thick black curtains and remove the tape from the windows. Everything seemed less claustrophobic then.

I remember parts of growing up during the war, but to me some of it seemed more like a game that reality. I guess for children it may be felt just like any other day apart from the odd buildings being bombed and hearing ladies crying more often. I also remember adults coming into our house to listen to the radio more than usual and then talking in hushed voices in the room at the front of our house which we called the front room, which was kept for special occasions.

We always made Christmas fun, even during the war years and Mum always made sure that we had gifts. Two of my elder brothers (Ron and Kenny) were twins and even at the young age I was I knew that they caused Mum and Dad a lot of trouble. They were like a double act of mischief, but never really meant anyone any harm. They would often be in trouble with the police for getting into fights, being brought home to our house and all the neighbours gawping out of the windows at our house to see what they had been up to this time. During the war years I remember that Ron and Kenny were always able to get hold of extra fruit and vegetables and meat for Mum and this was more so at Christmas. They also got hold of a pretty box of chocolates for Mum one year – don't know how, or where from, but I remember Mum treasured the box once it was empty for years and years until she passed away.

I remember the war years as not being all that bad really for me and I used to love going to the air raid shelter and meeting my friends there, it was fun. At Christmas we would all sing carols together and play games – sometimes it felt like there was no war at all, well to me anyway. I remember the fun of making paper Christmas decorations and hanging them up.

There were the sad times too, when my best friend Ida's older brother was killed by a falling wall that had been bombed. Shortly after that Ida and the rest of her family moved out of Eastbourne to the countryside somewhere up north as her Mum was not well by that point and they felt that the calmness of the country life would be good for her. Sadly, I never heard from Ida again and I would often wonder what she was doing.

Life was hard growing up during this time but it was also good too and made children appreciate the everyday small things a lot more. There was sadness, but there was also much joy too and I remember those days fondly and always will.

Women were always looking for new ways of running the home and the *English Woman's Domestic Magazine* which was published monthly from 1866 was the ideal way to keep up to date with all the latest household tips and trends and was a very popular read. Widows and poor ladies of the town could contact the Eastbourne Society for Promoting Female Industry, which was founded in 1861. The object of the society was to give employment to help them generate a small income for themselves and their families and it did so by supplying ladies with sewing work; the items made were then sold, generating an income. The society also often organised sales of useful clothing at the Trinity School Rooms to help raise much-needed funds.

Rhoda Cottingham (neé Hunt)

The following is an account of a woman's life in Eastbourne – it is quite a remarkable story, and was told to me by Mrs Janet Gadd. Janet explained that this is about her grandmother, Rhoda Matilda Hunt's life and struggle.

Rhoda Hunt was born in 1871 in either Steyning or Ringer, East Sussex to Mr John Hunt and Miss Lucy Ann Hillman. Her husband, Mr Daniel Cottingham was born 1871 in Arlington, East Sussex and was in the Navy from 1 May 1889, until the end of 1900.

Rhoda and Daniel met and married in 1903 in Hailsham, East Sussex. The couple made their home North Lodge, Folkington, East Sussex. They had a daughter, Lilian Mary, who was born on 8 December 1906.

Daniel sadly passed away in June 1913, and at that time the family were living in a small single storey building between the railway line and what is now known as the A27 road, opposite to the entrance to Folkington Farm. It is understood that Daniel was working on the farm in the stables attending to the leatherwork for the horses at Folkington Manor and Rhoda was employed repairing linens in the Manor House to the Gwynne family.

Because Rhoda would not hold the funeral when the Gwynne family told her to, as she wanted her relatives to be there and there was not time to arrange it, the Gwynne family would not let the horse and cart go directly up the farm road to the church, it had to go back towards Polegate and up Folkington Lane. Almost double the journey. Within a week, mother and daughter were out of the hovel which was demolished to make way for modern housing developments.

Janet's mother was sadly put into foster care, and when Rhoda went to see her early one evening, she was kneeling in bed, fast asleep, as the rags tied in her hair to make it curl were too tight for her to lie on her head. Rhoda took the rags out of her daughter's hair and took her away. There was very little support for women in Rhoda's position. Some had families that would take them in and look after them but many like Rhoda had to struggle.

Somehow, the next part of the story is that the pair of them moved into the Charles Jewell Working Women's Club, Eastbourne and they were living in the flat on the top floor of the building. Rhoda was the stewardess for the club from March 1915, until September 1942, some twenty-eight years. I once spoke to a woman who had known her, a lady called Jean who had lived nearby. Rhoda and Jean's family would meet on their weekly visit to the baths situated along Seaside and they became good friends. The building is now used by Eastbourne Operatic and Dramatic Society (EODS).

Jean explained that Rhoda made the most wonderful bread pudding, and that she was a very firm but fair woman. Janet was born in May 1941, in the flat, during an air raid and recalls being told many tales about Eastbourne being in doodlebug alley and of all the buildings which were destroyed during this time.

Janet also remembers being told that Rhoda organised whist drives events, coach outings all over the place, and dances at the town hall and was very much involved in the local community.

Janet's father was unable to go in the forces as his leg had not mended properly after a pit fall when he was a coal miner. She was 9 months old when her parents moved with her to a rented house in Lower Willingdon, Eastbourne. They were there a short time but because her father had bad attacks of cramp, they moved to another property not far away which was more suitable for them all.

Janet's grandmother came to live with them, as a guest in September 1942 when she retired, and died there in 1943 when Janet was 2 years old. The older Janet has become, the more she realises what a formidable lady her grandmother must have been. How many women in those times provided such a secure home for themselves and their child? Janet explained that her daughter's godmother and her husband were leaders in the Youth Club in later years. Just a coincidence. Janet thinks that her grandmother provided a social life to many women in the poorer end of Eastbourne and brought a little joy and happiness to many women of Eastbourne who sadly had very little enjoyment in their lives at this difficult time.

What an achievement!!!

Ada Ellen Bayly (known as Edna Lyall)

In 1884, the family of Edna Lyall (real name Ada Ellen Bayly) moved to Eastbourne. Born in Brighton in 1857, Edna was the youngest of four children; her brother became a clergyman and her sisters both married clergymen. Sadly, her parents both passed away before Edna was 14. Edna was an unwell child and this would follow her throughout her life. She was educated at home and then later at private schools in Brighton. Following school, she lived with her eldest sister for a while and moved with them when the family moved to a house at number 16 College Road, Eastbourne, which at the time was described as detached and gabled, with red tiling and covered with exquisite ivy and creepers and bathed in the shade of elm trees.

It was on the top floor of this house that Edna had her study and her writing room and it was here that she penned much of her work. From a young age she had wanted to be a writer and she had her first book, *Won by Waiting*, published in 1879. She wrote several titles before *We Two* in 1884, which was extensively reviewed in several publications including *The Spectator*. She spent a considerable amount of time writing and was successful, and is particularly known for her historical novels set in the seventeenth century. Her later writing took on social and political topics of the day including such subjects as Irish Home Rule, English Divorce Laws and sufferings of women during the Boer War.

Edna was a supporter of the Liberal Party and an active member of the Eastbourne Women's Liberal Association and worked tirelessly behind the scenes. Despite ill health she enjoyed travelling and exploring new places, including Norway, France and Italy and used her experiences in many of her novels. Edna passed away at the age of 45 at her College Road home. A long obituary in the *Eastbourne Gazette* for 11 February 1903, spoke of her work, her generosity and her sympathetic character.

Her writing style has been described as always clear and pleasant and that she was a great influence on popular thought and life. Edna was an inspiring writer who should not be forgotten and I am so pleased to have been able to include her in this book. Two of the newer churches of Eastbourne have memorials to Edna. The windows in St Peter's where she often worshipped, and the three bells at St Saviour's were donated by her and named Eric, Hugo and Donovan after three of her fictional characters.

The life of Elizabeth Quill (1861–1929) was an interesting one. She was better known as Kitty Quill from Kingstown, Ireland, and lived most of her time in London. However, she spent long summer months on the coast in Eastbourne selling flowers. She was married to David Quill with whom there were several reports of a volatile relationship. The Duke of Devonshire often had many guests to stay at Compton Place and in 1878 Queen Victoria's daughter was one of his guests for six weeks. Kitty Quill provided the flowers for the duration of her stay and became known as the Flower Seller. In 1891, Kitty and David made more permanent arrangements as they are on the census living at Tideswell Road, Eastbourne. Kitty established herself with a regular pitch on Eastbourne seafront for many years and became a well-known and much-loved local character, even appearing on local postcards of the town. She passed away in 1929 in Eastbourne.

Mr & Mrs Ann Pestel – Professional Photographers

In 1895, Mr Arthur Pestel, a photographer, moved with his wife, Mrs Ann Pestel, to 49 Terminus Road, Eastbourne and established a photographic studio where they worked together until Arthur's death in 1900 at the age of 32. Ann really came into her own following the death of her husband and continued to run a very successful business. It was rare for a woman to run a photographic studio at the time. Ann had the help of Ada Pestel, her late husband's unmarried sister; Ada helped Ann look after the children, whilst she worked long hours to make the business a success. In 1901–1902 the trade directory showed that Ann was the only female photographer listed out of a total of fourteen studios in Eastbourne. Ann also changed the spelling of her surname to Pestell and added 'Madame' to the title. It was not unusual for photography studios at the time to adopt this approach; it was considered highly desirable to give a sense of noble pedigree by adopting a French or continental-sounding name.

Madame Pestell's photographic images were no larger than postcard size, however they were then pasted and mounted for the finished portrait to be displayed. The photographic business ran in the family and by 1911, Ann's son, Arthur Robert Pestel, had started work at the Terminus Road studio and the 1911 census records show Arthur Pestel as a 17-year-old photographer's apprentice.

By the 1920s, Madame Pestell's images had increased in size and many showed a different style than had previously been seen. The National Trust own a collection of her work and these have been displayed in many of their houses listed as '*by Madame Pestell of Eastbourne*'.

Between 1925 and 1930, Madame Pestell moved her portrait studio from 49 Terminus Road to 7 Victoria Place and she finally retired in 1931 in her early sixties.

Marjorie Frances Bruford (1902–1958)

Better known as 'Midge', Marjorie was born in Eastbourne and was well known as an artist. She was the daughter of A.W. Bruford and it was her father who encouraged Midge to paint and to take up a career in the arts. Midge studied in Newlyn and in Paris but spent most of her life in Cornwall; she never married and spent her time supporting numerous artists. She was best known for her landscape paintings and oil portraits. Bruford was a regular exhibitor at the Royal Academy, having some thirty-two works in total accepted for display there between 1924 and 1955. She joined the St Ives Society of Artists in 1938 and remained a member until she passed away in 1958.

With consumer spending increasing more and more during this period, women were looking at ways to make being a housewife a little easier and this brought about new kitchen equipment and gadgets on to the market, including utensils for practical everyday cooking or baking and electric toasters, which made their way from the USA. Men were still the main workers in the family, bringing home the wage, with the women staying at home and cooking and cleaning for the family. Even at times such as Christmas the women of the family were expected to cook the meal and clean up afterwards, while the men would traditionally go to a football match during the afternoon of Christmas Day.

Television became increasingly popular during the 1950s which opened a whole new and exciting world. At the start of the decade less than 10 per cent of the population had a TV, by the end of the 1950s, this had increased to 75 per cent.

Elizabeth David (1913–1992) - Professional Writer

Elizabeth is best known for her contribution to cookery writing, which had national and international appeal. She was born at Wootton Manor, close to Eastbourne and her father Rupert Gwynne was Conservative MP for Eastbourne (1911–1924). She was a restless and rebellious young woman and in 1939 she travelled across Europe with her married lover. In 1944, she met and married Lieutenant Colonel Anthony David, an officer in the Indian Army with whom she travelled to New Delhi. However, she soon grew bored of India and after becoming ill in 1946 decided to return to England.

She returned to a very different Britain from the one she had left. Rationing was still in place, meaning produce and items were difficult to get hold of and meals were uninspiring. Elizabeth had grown used to cooking basic Mediterranean food and had collected vast notes about the recipes she created. It was now that Elizabeth started to try and create some of the delicious food she had encountered whilst in Europe. When her husband returned from India in 1947, they moved to a house in Chelsea in which Elizabeth lived for the rest of her life. The move opened new opportunities for Elizabeth and she found herself writing for magazines such as *Harper's Bazaar* – her first article for this was 1000 words published in March 1949, called 'Rice again'. Even though it was still very difficult to get hold of much of the Mediterranean produce Elizabeth craved, her European travels and exploits meant she could open a new culinary world to readers and alter attitudes to food, which was refreshing at a time of austerity. She continued writing for *Harper's Bazaar* for a further six years. In 1950 *A Book of Mediterranean Food* was published and following its success Elizabeth was asked to write about French cooking. Her next book, *French Country Cooking* was published in 1951. She continued writing prolifically, introducing exciting and tasty cuisine to the previously bland diet of much of the population of Britain. An inspiring lady.

An interesting advert appeared in the *Sussex Agricultural Express* of 1949 as follows:

> *Eastbourne Hospital Management Committee, St Mary's Hospital, Eastbourne. Head cook required, male or female. Wages £6/15/- per week basic male, £5/8/- per week female, plus rates for working Sundays. Residence can be provided for female applicant for which a charge will be made. Apply to the catering officer immediately.*

An advert placed the previous year in the *West Sussex Gazette* in 1948 read:

> *Miscellaneous vacancies at Gildredge Tuberculosis Hospital required immediately. 6 RN required (non-resident) also State Enrolled Assistant Nurses (non-resident). Salaries according to experience and scale.*

Adverts such as this offer us a glimpse into otherwise lesser-known histories and stories of a given time and place. They are primary sources and give an insight into life, work and other aspects of life which we may not know about. Adverts for jobs can give an indication as to the pay and working conditions of the time – enabling us to compare costs of living and pay with our own today. They offer us a unique first-hand record of a snippet of history.

The time had come for changes in how women worked, and having experienced and learned new skills during the Second Word War, many now wanted so much more than they had previously had as they realised the opportunities which were now available to them.

CHAPTER THREE

Family Life: 'Home Sweet Home'

If there is one area of women's struggle which has changed the most I believe it to be marriage and divorce. For so long women had suffered at the hands of husbands who showed them no love or affection in a marriage that was more to do with status (certainly for the middle and upper classes) rather than a loving relationship. It was the time to start looking at ways to help women who were living distressing existences and to be able to offer them an alternative. Courts had introduced ways to make it easier for women to divorce their husbands. It was still very rare for a woman to do so, but it was not impossible. However, with women handing over monies and any other wealth on marriage, very few Victorian women had their own means, which meant that the divorce would have to be paid for by their husband.

Before 1857, Victorian England was an unjust place for a married woman. A man could take all the earnings and inheritance from his wife. Divorce cases were managed by the Church of England which made divorce a formidable difficulty, unless the lady was extremely wealthy. Under the Matrimonial Causes Act of 1857, women divorcing on the grounds of adultery not only had to prove their husbands had been unfaithful, but also had to prove additional faults, which included cruelty, rape and incest, making the whole process very distressing for the wife involved.

Social and political laws were dictating women's freedom to take independent decisions about marriage and employment. Even the fashions of the time put emphasis on men's authority and control. Long and heavy dresses which scraped the floor along with tight, boned corsets meant that these 'married' women would struggle to move. Behind all the glamour, these dresses embodied the imprisoned bodies under the unjust society of Victorian England, especially after a woman was married.

The 1857 Matrimonial Causes Act was a small stepping stone to freedom even though it was very limited. A private members' bill in 1923 made it easier for women to petition for divorce for adultery, but it still had to be proved. Moving forward to 1937, the law was changed and divorce was allowed on other grounds including drunkenness, insanity and desertion.

Fashion and Shops in Eastbourne

Images carried by the *London Illustrated News* in 1842 opened the world of fashion to many ladies up and down the country. As the newspaper was available nationally, it spread the popular new fashions and styles emerging from the fashion world. Ladies were also able to order these items from London.

When Queen Victoria opened the Great Exhibition on 1 May 1851, she unleashed a new fashion statement. She wore a headdress of feathers and this was to start a new following in bird feathers on clothing, millinery and accessories. This craze was considered by many as barbaric due to the way in which some birds were captured and had their feathers removed in the name of fashion. It was estimated that tens of thousands of birds lost their lives to fund this fashion and many people were prepared to fight for the birdlife. In Manchester in 1889, ladies who felt very strongly about the use of birds in fashion formed a group known as the 'Fur, Fin and Feather Group', their mission was to stop killing for fashion. This group continues to this day and is now known as the Royal Society for the Protection of Birds (RSPB).

Queen Victoria had huge influence over what women of the time wore and she was very much aware of how she dressed and how it was perceived by the population. However, for her wedding she went against the normal tradition of wearing the royal robes and wore a white wedding dress; the beginning of what we know of today as the traditional colour for most wedding dresses. She was very interested in fashion and the power that fashion gave the wearer. Queen Victoria was always the supporter of British products and would always wear British when she attended state events. She was also obsessed with theatre and would often have her guests dressed a certain way for an event they were to attend, while she would wear a completely different outfit and colour – thus giving out a message of power. Following the death of Queen Victoria's husband, Prince Albert, in 1861, many women took on the mourning dress of Queen Victoria by remaining in black for the rest of their lives. Many businesses benefited greatly from this new fashion. After a period of wearing black, less harsh colours could be introduced such as grey or lilac. Mourning was an enormous business in the Victorian period as it also required for lavish announcements to be placed in newspapers, mourning cards detailing the death, stationery with black edges and also special mourning jewellery, often made from Whitby jet.

There were many large and well-respected drapers and outfitters in Eastbourne and one such store was known as Evenden's, The Fashion Drapers. In an advertisement in the *Eastbourne Gazette*, 1913, the store had almost a full-page advertisement promoting their sale:

Evenden's Sale of Great Importance

The Directors have decided to enlarge and develop still further their show room and fashion departments which show continued expansion and greater accommodation to cope with the present demand for Ready to Wear goods.

A great sale will therefore be held of the stock of:

China and Glass

Soft Furnishings

Dresses and Silks

Which must be cleared to provide additional space.

NO WINDOWS will be dressed during the first days of sale.

Irresistible Non-Repeat Bargains in all Depts.

Ladies are invited to come early it will be a great money saving event!

Bobby & Co Ltd. of Terminus Road, Eastbourne was also a well-established family run business with stores along the south-east coast. The *Eastbourne Gazette* often carried large advertisements in its pages promoting for example the best of ladies' wear:

Summer Smartness

Delightfully portrayed in a new collection of Gowns for Ascot

An ecru and black lace combination to make this becoming gown for the young matron. It is finished with diamante on the corsage and is suitable for dinner or more formal occasions.

Price 6 ½ Gns

Bobby's also offered something new to ladies of the town by opening a credit account, which the store liked to say, 'Makes Shopping so much easier'.

Henry Playfair Ltd. was a well-known shoe shop at 120 Seaside Road, Eastbourne and in 1943, they also reminded the local people that they were still in business despite the recent air raids on the Seaside area.

There was a wonderful talk entitled 'clothes and character', given by the actress Miss Eva Moore to the women of Eastbourne in 1926 and reported in the *Yorkshire Evening Post* newspaper. The advice this lady gave was to do with wearing skirts and how to choose the correct one for your shape. Her advice was to stand in front of your mirror and see what sort of legs you have. If they are shapely then you can afford to wear a short skirt, however the shorter length should be avoided if you have large calves. For this shape you should wear your skirts a further 5 or 6 inches longer. Miss Moore was a popular actress of the time and the talk was well-received by the local women.

There was an article written in 1920 for a new fashion magazine which said:

A society bride a few weeks back was venturesome enough to go to the altar wearing a dress of peacock blue. Silver leaves held the bridal veil of blue tulle, it was a startling innovation and the result was extraordinarily effective.

During the 1920s and into the following decade, Dale and Kerley's department store thrived in a prominent position at the corner of Terminus Road and Seaside in the centre of Eastbourne. Dale and Kerley's was one of four top-end shops in the town which specialised in top of the range products and the luxury market. Daily tea dances were held for the ladies of the town each weekday afternoon in the top floor restaurant. During the Second World War the building was used for making parachutes and took a direct hit during bombing of the town, which resulted in the building being rebuilt after the end of the war. Today Dale and Kerley's is better known as T.J. Hughes and is a popular addition to the numerous shops that Eastbourne has to offer.

Home Sweet Home in Eastbourne

The Eastbourne area has always had a rural community with farming villages dotted across the Downs. Sadly, today, much of what was once farmland has been developed for housing. Remnants of the past still linger with the odd farmworkers' cottages remaining here and there, offering a glimpse of what life was once like.

In 1919, the first council houses were built in Eastbourne. They were built on 140 acres of land off Victoria Drive and provided much-needed family homes for people of the town. During this period there was a lack of servants available around the town, due to more girls going into mills and factory work and therefore ladies of the house were looking for simple ways of filling the mouths of their families and, more importantly, with food that they could cook. For many of the middle and upper classes, this was the first time they had had to think about cooking and providing meals for their families. Within two days of the declaration of war in 1914, the cost of provisions rocketed upwards. Newspapers swapped their usual high-class fashions pages full of tips and advice on the latest gowns and accessories to address the needs of the women of the day and help provide them with ideas and recipes for cheap meals and easy-to-make soups.

No one thought that the war would continue for as long as it did and, with some of the wealthiest families consuming more than their fair share of meat, the supplies were exhausted very quickly. Something had to be done and so the idea of the allotment was born. People could rent a piece of land to grow and cultivate their own fruit and vegetables at a time where there was little available.

1918 saw the introduction of rationing. Meat coupons were given to the population and other items were also available only in very reduced numbers. For many families it was a matter of making the best of what you had and what was available – which a lot of the time was not the best. However, this made women use only what had to be used and in a variety of ways in order to get the best from an item. It is often said that war years sometimes see a population eating better than at times of peace.

Exploring the villages and hamlets of this area can turn up many stories about what life used to be like and none more so that than of Lady Isabella Elizabeth Turnour who lived close to the village of Berwick, on the South Downs. It is said that she saw 100 years of life, living in the Victorian era and living it out. She and her sister Catherine found life to be uneventful as they chose to live as unmarried ladies, but they took a vivid interest in life in the village and were involved in activities and events such as fetes and parties for the local people. They knew everything about the area, the names and the family history of all the tenants and servants. They also knew the name of every field and wood of the area and could describe in detail, all the birds, trees and plants found in the country around their home. They kept a journal record of the rainfall and the sunshine, recording in detail the weather types of each day, rainfall, wind direction and how much sunlight fell on their house each day. They also recorded the nature around them and how this changed with the seasons. Lady Elizabeth recalled a visit to Hastings when she was just 4 years old, before the start of the Victorian era. She sat between her parents on the front seat of a phaeton, a valet and a maid sat behind them. A groom rode with them, leading a spare horse.

Changes happened when those who had experienced great wealth from the land were suddenly faced with cheap corn from America and so the demand for English corn plummeted. There followed twenty years' depression in this area. For the families who had built their fortunes off the land this was devastating. They had to find other ways to make money. Some looked to sell their property, while others had their sons head to the city or had their daughters marry into wealthy families who were the new and prosperous industrialists.

The wealthy were not the only ones affected, the poor also suffered. Many who had worked all their lives on the land, and knew only farm work, were forced to leave the countryside for the towns and cities to look for work and this brought problems of its own. The population of London grew from 3.9 million in 1871 to 7.3 million by 1911. It was during the 1890s and the 1900s that the first provision of municipal flats for the poor were seen, although with the vast numbers of people moving to the cities, these were often overcrowded and with that came more problems; a distinct lack of good housing for this growing population together with unsanitary living conditions, inadequate health care and disease.

Those who were successful and able to progress from the working class to middle class had a huge effect on housing. In addition, as their education improved so did the jobs they could get and thus they adopted middle-class aspirations. One sign of respectability was a decent home.

During the Victorian era, the large and dark houses were gloomy and uncomfortable and following Queen Victoria's death, people wanted something else. The population's attitudes had changed and they were now looking to the future rather than staying in the dark Victorian era which they had done for so long. If they worked hard and brought home good money, they wanted to enjoy their homes and not live in an outdated era. The population wanted affordable and manageable homes within travelling distance of their place of work in the towns and cities.

The 'flat' was starting to become more acceptable and many families aspired to call one their home. Flats had been seen in the past as squalid accommodation for the poorer classes of society, however as times were changing, flats were becoming more appealing to more of the working and middle classes with the benefits a flat could bring them, such as a shorter commute to work or being able to live in a property which was clean, warm and above all secure. Magazines of the time had articles and advertisements for flats and maisonettes and how to live in this new style of dwelling and how to make the most from furnishing them.

A new style of city was also being designed and these sprung up in the Midlands in the form of Garden Cities. Neat and green cities within commutable distance of London which offered everyone peace and tranquillity and style. These new cities appealed greatly to the Edwardians with their fresh air and health obsessions. Eastbourne was one such town which was designed to make the most of its position and to offer a unique genteel seaside living experience for residents. The streets were laid out around green spaces, offering clean air away from the city life which many residents had moved away from.

Tall Victorian terraced houses were no longer fashionable, with their endless stairs which took forever to clean and required an army of servants. After the First World War was declared, cheap servants became harder to find as many were called up to work in the war effort. This resulted in owners of the larger houses being unable to cope with maintaining a large property and numbers of them were demolished to make way for smaller houses and apartments, which were easier and cheaper to run.

One of the most dramatic changes in terms of interior design to affect this period was the growing use of a sitting room or living hall. The Arts and Crafts Movement instigated this change in living style, calling for a more relaxed and informal way of living with a return to a simpler style. The living hall was to be an area where you could welcome a weary traveller or friend, and where you could remove your outdoor clothing.

Today there is a vast housing stock in the town and suburbs of Eastbourne which stretches along the coast in both an easterly and westerly direction to Pevensey and Brighton. There is little to distinguish between the towns of this area now as there was once vast marshland and farmland, much of which has been built on. Space for new housing is at a premium in these coastal areas and this has been pretty much the case since 1919 when more land was acquired on the north-west side of the borough when a housing scheme was set up. It was reported in the *Coventry Evening Telegraph* of 1919 that Eastbourne Town Council decided to put in an offer of £15,000 for 140 acres of freehold building land from Lord Willingdon's Ratton Estate. This land would provide space to construct some one thousand homes and would also provide allotments and small holdings.

The area of Eastbourne has always been popular with people from all walks of life and has attracted many people from other parts of the United Kingdom and further afield. Much of the elegant and grand housing close to the seafront was taken up with guest houses and hotels and for educational establishments. This meant that the housing possibilities for that area had to be located elsewhere in and around the town and this saw the proposals for numerous housing estates being built to provide homes for workers and families alike who wished to call Eastbourne their home.

An article in the *Sussex Agricultural Express* of 1947 reported that the:

COUNTY BOROUGH OF EASTBOURNE PERMANENT HOUSING Corporation invites tenders for the erection of one block of four houses of traditional construction in Kingston Road, Hampden Park, Eastbourne.

Applications for tender forms and Bills of Quantities must be delivered to the Borough Surveyor, 2/4, Saffrons Road, Eastbourne on or before the 17th May, 1947, and must be accompanied by a deposit cheque for £2 2s 0d payable to the Eastbourne Corporation. The deposit will be returned on receipt [of] a bona-fide tender. Tender forms and Bills of Quantities will be forwarded to applicants on or about the 21st May, 1947. Tenders on the forms provided and enclosed in sealed envelopes bearing the words "Tender for Houses" but not bearing any words or marks indicating the senders, must be delivered to the undersigned not later than 5 p.m. on the 14th day after the day on which the tender forms and Bills of Quantities are despatched by the Borough Surveyor to applicants for them. The lowest or any tenders will not necessarily be accepted. F. H. BUSBY, Town Clerk. Town Hall. Eastbourne. 6th May. 1947.

Women of the time had all manner of magazines and books, such as *Odhams Home Cookery Illustrated, Practical Home Mending Made Easy,* and *The Pictorial Guide to Modern Home Needlecraft* describing how to make the ideal home in this new style and how to create the all-important atmosphere in this part of the house. Lots of women wanted to adopt the new way of living and the new values that went with it and to be looked upon as modern, having left the Victorian dark ages long behind them.

Billiard rooms were popular for middle and upper classes of this time and men would often retire following a meal to the billiard room. Billiards was such a popular sport that every house had to have a billiard table and if the house was too small to accommodate one then there were special table tops which could be made so that the game could still be played on the temporary surface.

Libraries were also an essential part of the Edwardian home which consisted of good lighting and a writing desk. At first, libraries appeared to be quite masculine but over time magazines and journals recommended the addition of flowers and photographs and pieces of china to make it feel softer.

The Edwardians carried forward their love of bright sunshine and airiness to their bedrooms. Painted in light, pale colours the Edwardian bedroom was a place of quiet retreat with flowers in particular adorning the walls and textiles of the day.

It was, however, the change in the kitchens and bathrooms during this period that brought about the biggest change to women's lives. There had been cholera to contend with in previous years but there had been many advances in medicine with people having a greater understanding of health and well-being. Everyone became obsessed with cleanliness and hygiene. Walls were painted white so that they could be kept clean and repainted and the corners of the walls in the kitchen had their corners rounded like those in hospitals so that germs and disease did not fester there. Tiles were used in areas such as behind the sink and the range so that they could be kept clean and free of old food. Wooden floors were covered with a linoleum substance or replaced with stones, again to reduce any bacteria from spreading throughout the home.

Electricity was slowly being introduced in the 1910s and most households in Edwardian England still used gas ranges to cook on. The kitchen had built-in dressers for storing cooking utensils and other items of everyday use, and food was kept in the larder which was made of marble and wooden shelves. Some larger houses had separate larders for milk and meat so that they could always be kept apart.

Much of the previously unobtainable delights of interior design were now available for Edwardians at all levels and were easily in reach of the middle classes. Books and journals gave demonstration and instructions on how to embroider lamp shades and make other simple items for the home. Wallpaper meant that walls which were by far from perfect could be covered to give a new appearance, but the colour and style of a room could be changed with minimal cost and without having to change the furniture. It meant that it was easier and cheaper for Edwardian women to keep their houses cleaner.

The rapid industrialisation of England during the Victorian and Edwardian period brought about a change in location for a large section of the population. Many of these people found themselves living some distance away from a parish church, which had been a major part of their spiritual life. As well as the physical barriers this brought, many people also felt distanced from the established church. There were, during the eighteenth and nineteenth century, periods when the clergy was drawn from the ranks of the gentry, and social hierarchy was evident within the walls of the church. The strict seating arrangements in churches were based upon class, which did more to alienate many of the population, who in turn started to look elsewhere for somewhere to worship.

Uniform became a part of life for millions of British women, from bus attendants to the Land Army. Employers took women from all walks of life and, for many, being given a uniform meant they were better dressed during the war than they had been previously.

Priscilla Mann, from Eastbourne, remembers how her mum used to talk about seeing the young ATS and WAAF women dressed so elegantly in their uniforms during wartime and how, secretly, she was envious of how glamorous they looked – especially as clothes for civilians were rationed and hard to come by. Priscilla recalls her mum talking about how she and her sister would search through the house to try and find something to use to make their old worn out clothes better and more fashionable, and how upset the two sisters often were when they could not get hold of their favourite beauty products and had to substitute items of make-up with things such as beetroot juice for rouge.

Clothes rationing continued after the war and Britain remained on an economic downturn. However, bit by bit, the Parisian fashion houses started to reopen and in 1947 Christian Dior launched a new collection of extravagant clothes using yards and yards of material; this extravagance caused a storm because it was a time of austerity and items were scarce. This new style accentuated curves and brought back a sense of romance and beauty during the later 1940s and ladies loved it. This also came at a time when bold colours and beachwear were being designed, and with inspiration from American styles also entering the British market, things were set to change like never before. These new styles and colours were a much-welcomed change to the drab shades and styles which many had put up with for so long. There was a strong feeling about fashion at this time: many loved it, but equally many hated it, viewing it as frivolous and wasteful after the rationing and deprivation of the war and for many, the hardships they had suffered were still very raw. However, these new styles became a symbol of the return to prosperity and a new sort of 'normal' life. Women could start to feel feminine and glamorous again. Women who for so long had hidden away and made do with cast-offs and hand-me-downs, could now feel reborn in these new fashions and the confidence the clothes gave them.

The war also brought social and cultural change as women took on more and greater responsibilities and roles both at home and at work, resulting in greater numbers of women entering the workplace. Slacks, once considered scandalous and fit only for the boudoir, gained popularity. For many years however, even into the 1960s, it was to be a subject of debate as to whether they were appropriate in the workplace or not! And even if they should be worn by women at all.

After the war, the younger generation increasingly favoured stylish comfortable separates, rather than dresses which seemed to have become the national dress for women of all ages. Tops and bottoms were the dress of the modern woman, being able to interchange items and mix designs in a way like never before.

During this tough decade, 1940's Britain looked to foreign places, such as France, for food inspiration and influences, and crepes were hugely popular. More hotels, especially those on the coast like Eastbourne, were serving dishes from Europe to their guests and so these ideas filtered down to the households of the towns. Salads became popular in this period, although they were drowned in Heinz Salad Cream, a bestseller at the time.

The modern home of the late 1940s could expect to have cold running water both in the kitchen and in the bathroom. Small boilers (coal- and gas-fired) or electric immersion heaters could be installed to provide some hot running water.

Edwardian bridal group showing the fashionable hemline of the time.

Edwardian fashions.

Two friends displaying late 1940s, early 1950s fashion.

Group of ladies on a visit to parkland close to Eastbourne.

Above left: *Photo by J Berryman – photographer to the queen – showing Victorian dress.*

Above right: *Photo by G and R Lavis, an Eastbourne based photography business.*

Beachy Head, Eastbourne

Marine Parade, Eastbourne

Postcard showing two popular areas of Eastbourne, dated 1918. Beachy head (above) and Marine Parade (below).

Postcard of the Grand Hotel, clearly illustrating how the hotel received its name.

Old photograph in the form of a postcard of the old All Saints Hospital.

Postcard dated 1955 showing the band stand and Eastbourne pier in all their glory. The message on the back reads, 'Enjoying a nice comfortable holiday here'.

Terminus Road, Eastbourne (undated). This was the road that visitors who arrived in town by the railway would have walked down from the station.

'This is the house that man built'. Anti-suffrage propaganda.

EASTBOURNE

I wish you good luck and good cheer,
And send you my greeting.
Here are some views, and you'll agree,
They want some beating

'Good Luck from Eastbourne'. Postcard from 1927 which folds out to show photographic black and white images of Eastbourne.

Lady wearing fur to keep warm on the sea front. Fur was fashionable at the time.

Right: *Portrait of Rhoda Cottingham, taken 1937.*

Below: *A dance at the Town Hall in Eastbourne, organised by Rhoda. Her son-in-law can be seen on the extreme left wearing a bow tie, his wife in front of him.*

Above: *Taken at the Charles Jewell premises, Seaside Eastbourne. Rhoda is in the centre with her daughter to the left, behind her.*

Left: *Rhoda pictured with a friend.*

Rhoda Cottingham holding her granddaughter in her lap, with her daugher, Lilian, standing around. Taken around 1941 on the Charles Jewell premises.

Rhoda Cottingham

Left: *Rhoda, presumedly on a coach trip.*

Below: *Group photo. Winnie Etherington in front in the light dress with Rhoda behind her.*

Rhoda Cottingham on the left with Mrs Lambert and Mrs Merritt. The 4th lady is unknown at the time of printing.

Rhoda's retirement certificate presentation.

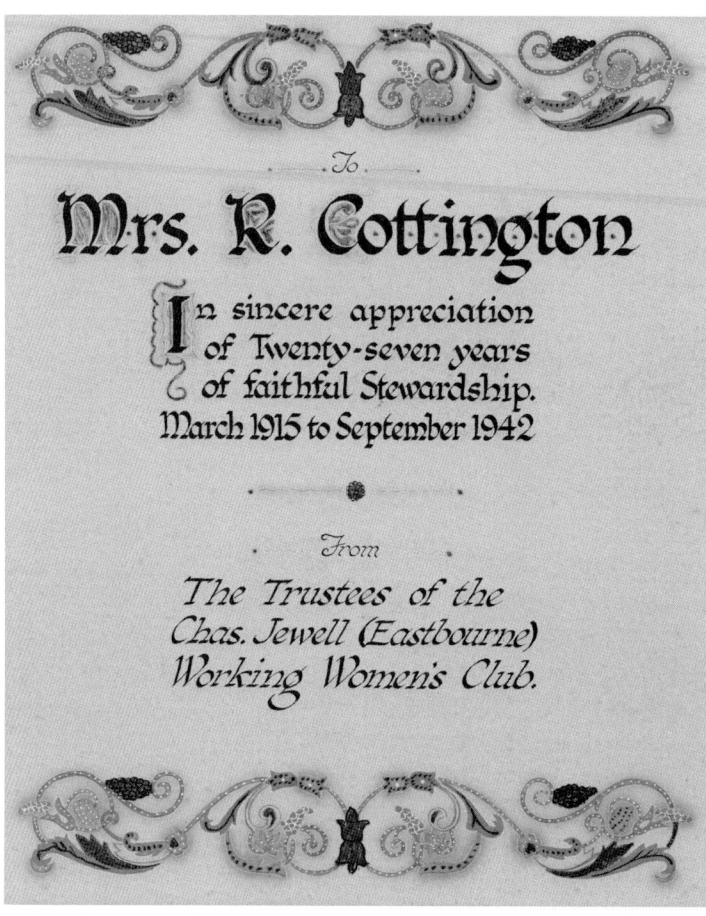

_To_

Mrs. R. Cottington

In sincere appreciation
of Twenty-seven years
of faithful Stewardship.
March 1915 to September 1942

From

The Trustees of the
Chas. Jewell (Eastbourne)
Working Women's Club.

Left: _Leaving certificate that was awarded to Rhoda Cottingham in 1942 for twenty-seven years of faithful stewardship._

Below: _Camp Journal, April 1916. Some of the cooks at Summerdown Camp with a poem about them._

Summerdown Camp. The camp was set up in the First World War for wounded and ill service men. Image kindly provided by East Dean and Friston Local History Group.

XXXX.

Above and left: *The elegant Grand Hotel, Eastbourne.*

Home life was challenging for families during the war years and the rationing of food continued into the 1950s, making everyday meals a challenge for any housewife, let alone at Christmas. The general idea was that families had to 'make do' and be very creative with very little. One item in the cupboard which was not rationed was sherry! So this would have been used to add to baked fruits and maybe the housewife would have indulged in the odd glass or two while trying to think up of an appetising dish for Christmas.

What must it have been like to have been a housewife during the war years? And how did they cope with so little when compared with today's standards?

With the new style of houses and bungalows popping up on the edges of towns, many labour-saving, new technologies were also making their way into the homes of the modern women of the time. Some areas of the country were suffering from hardship, however much of the south-east was doing well. Many people in the south-east had work, and with that came the change of a new modern home and new products to make life that little bit easier.

Something which brought huge change to the lives of thousands of women – which may seem quite a small thing by today's standards – was the electric iron. This was by far the most popular of all electric items from the late 1930s throughout the war years. These new irons were quick, clean and easy, and gave the housewife faced with her pile of ironing more time to pursue other tasks around the home.

One companion that many housewives and families had during the war years was the radio. Although not that new, it was a lifeline for many during the war when there was little or no other means of contact with loved ones who were away. Many women felt isolated being left at home to look after the children, not knowing if their husbands would return from the war, and so the radio was a friend to them, bringing some ease from the stress and worries of life at the time.

One thing which did change in all homes up and down the country was the use of the garden. Prior to the war, gardens were neatly planted with roses and all manner of flowers, but this changed when every inch of garden was required for growing food. Flower gardens were a luxury which Britain could not afford and it was the opinion of most of the population that good garden soil should be used for growing vegetables and fruit, not flowers. There were many gardening programmes that were keenly listened to on the radio; *The Wireless Gardener* was a popular Sunday afternoon show which played to enormous audiences. Mr Cecil Henry Middleton's advice on his show *In Your Garden* helped millions of people to get the most out of their gardens at this very hard time. He was one of the first radio presenters on the subject dedicated to gardening.

Through Mr Middleton's advice, people were encouraged to dig up every available piece of land and grow food in it. Aerial photographs of the time showed just how much people took this to heart. Not only were front and back gardens dug up, but roadside verges and railway cuttings, parks and public gardens and school playing fields were all turned over to the production of food. People also started to learn about year-round crops rather than just having a supply of food in the summer months. There was plenty of advice from such organisations as the Royal Horticultural Society (RHS) about how to get the most from gardens and what to plant and when.

The growing of tomatoes was particularly encouraged due to their high nutritional value and you only had to follow some simple rules to obtain a great crop. Families embraced these new ideas and looked forward to the challenge of growing their own food. Not only could the tomatoes be used in salads, but they could also be used in chutneys and sauces to last a family through the winter months.

Many herbs and traditional medicines had only been available from abroad before the war but now, with the uptake in growing at home, the plants would be far more readily available.

Stinging nettles were also a vegetable substitute and used as a useful additional wartime ingredient. Another spice grown was mustard, which, when crushed could be turned into a chest plaster for treating chest and cough-related ailments. Accounts of mustard plasters often turning up in wartime accounts of life due to ancient tales of cures for common chest complaints.

Wartime wages helped a lot of people to increase their standards of living since most family members of working age would be in work thus enabling them to be able to purchase their food rations.

Rationing was confusing and it was put in place to set a limit on how much people could buy. A typical weekly ration for one adult was 4oz bacon and ham, 12oz of sugar, 2oz tea, 1oz cheese, 2oz of preserves, 2oz cooking fat and 4oz butter. Meat was allocated by price and initially you could purchase up to the value of 1s 10d. Many in the countryside did not feel the pinch of rationing as much as the population did in the towns and cities. In the countryside, the opportunities for illicitly acquiring food beyond the ration quota were many and varied.

Many people living in the countryside took to foraging for foods such as mushrooms and berries to supplement their diets and even such items as dandelion leaves were used to bring colour and nutrition to salads.

Jam was a staple of food in pre-war Britain and remained so throughout the war years. It had huge significance far beyond what it has in our modern lives today. The energy that could be obtained from such small amounts of sugar led to its popularity with all classes of people, even the poorest. Many a teatime would be bread and jam rather than the previously popular bread and dripping. Jam could always be fallen back on, as everyone had the ingredients or a jar in the larder to help in times of need. With sugar being rationed, alternatives were sought and syrup and saccharin were the most common.

This typical wartime recipe for jam makes 4 jars:

4lb cooked fruit

1lb sugar

40 saccharin tablets

4 packs of gelatine (enough to set 4 pints of liquid)

1. *Stir the sugar into the cooked fruit pulp.*

2. *Dissolve the saccharin tablets in a little hot water and stir thoroughly into the sweetened fruit.*

3. *Pour into sterilised jars and allow to set.*

Apparently, this recipe doesn't taste that great, but at a time when ingredients were in short supply then you had to create the best you could from few ingredients.

Another favourite of the time was canned apples. All that was required were apples, salt and sugar. The process was simple:

1. *Peel and core the apples and place them into salted water to stop them from browning.*

2. *Meanwhile, prepare the sugar syrup mix by mixing together the sugar and water in a saucepan and bring to the boil.*

3. *Put as much of the prepared fruit into the cans as you can.*

4. *Pour the boiling syrup over the fruit in the can, leaving 1/4 inch from the top. Place a lid on top and a label on the front.*

5. *Now, most importantly, you must sterilise the fruit. Submerge the newly sealed can up to its neck in water, bringing the water slowly up to the boil and simmering for exactly eighteen minutes to kill any bacteria inside.*

6. *Once sterilised, leave to cool.*

Many of us like to eat familiar food at times of stress and turn to our favourites which we know will offer some comfort. So, what did housewives do during wartime when the usual ingredients were not available? Well, they had to be creative and make things out of unlikely sources. Fish and chips had become a very popular meal once a week pre-war, however during the war, it was not something that could be easily found and so an alternative sprung up in tips and recipes for those housewives still wishing to create this teatime treat.

It was called Mock Fish. Many fishermen had been called up to serve in the navy so fish was scarce and this would have been a welcome substitute.

This following recipe serves 2-3.

½ pint of milk, plus a little extra for brushing.

2oz ground rice

1 teaspoon chopped onion or leek

A spoonful of margarine about the size of a walnut

Anchovy essence (to season)

1 beaten egg

Handful of breadcrumbs.

1. *Pour the milk into a pan and bring it to the boil. Add the ground rice, chopped onion or leek, the margarine and the anchovy essence.*

2. *Let this simmer gently for twenty minutes, then take the pan off the stove, and stir in the beaten egg. Mix this together well and then transfer to a flat dish and spread the mixture out, 7-8 inches in diameter.*

3. *Cut the pieces the size and shape of fish fillets, brush with milk and roll in breadcrumbs. Fry until golden brown. Serve with parsley sauce and potatoes (if you were lucky enough to have some).*

The *Women's World* column in the *Eastbourne Herald* from 1946 reports that many local housewives attended the cookery demonstration at the Gas Company Theatre and many of them were eager to purchase the cook book afterwards. Miss Trench, the cookery demonstrator had avoided the use of eggs, making her recipes practical and economical. It was reported that she demonstrated a clever use of rabbit for a stew and in a pie. Miss Trench also showcased suet dumplings and lemonade to her audience.

Mrs Aileen Turnbull, recalls how hard it was growing up in the 1930s and the 1940s and she recalls some of the events of that period of her life:

> *Our family was large, I had three sisters and ten brothers and I was born in 1933. Mum had had two miscarriages in the two years prior to giving birth to me and I think it was due to this reason why Mum never really showed me any real affection. It was hard growing up in a family like this. When I look back at Mum's life, it was one of being pregnant pretty much for fifteen years without much of a break. The moment she recovered from one pregnancy, she was pregnant again. This was a huge strain on her health and well-being.*
>
> *I was not really brought up by Mum. She was more of a 'mother' than a mum and she was very strict. Her own upbringing had been very strict and she would have adopted much of what life had been like for her.*

Aileen described how she was mainly brought up by her two older sisters, Vera and Violet and she remembers seeing the affection which her mum gave to these two older siblings.

Aileen did not feel that she could ask her mum anything and she recalled the horrid day when her period arrived for the first time. 'I felt like I was dying – no one had talked to me about such things and Mum would not have dreamed about discussing such things with me, I had to ask my older sister Vera what was happening and she explained everything to me and made me feel so much better. It was a horrific experience for a young girl.' Aileen also remembers how difficult it was when any member of the family was unwell as they had to go and send for the doctor and pay him to come and see whoever was ill.

Aileen remembers being sent to school and hating every moment of it and would not do her written work. She said that she hated maths and would often get the cane across her hands for not being able to do what the teacher gave her to do. Aileen said that she hated her schooldays and could not wait to leave.

One thing which Aileen really looked forward to was when her cousin came to visit. Aileen's cousin was also called Violet (same as her elder sister) and would visit Aileen and the rest of the family a couple of times a month and they would have tea together. Aileen explained how she would get so excited when her cousin came to the house as she was like a breath of fresh air. Violet worked at a theatre as a chorus line dancer in another town, but close by enough to visit. She was about six years older than Aileen and so Aileen looked up to her. Violet worked in many major productions, which took her all over the country, appearing at glamorous theatres and piers. Violet's work meant that she often had dresses which were no longer any good to her and so she would offer them to Aileen when she visited. Even though these dresses were not new, to Aileen they meant the world. To an 8- or 9-year-old girl, in a time which was difficult for families, to be given these brightly coloured, glamorous dresses was like a dream come true. Even though they were too large for her, she had great fun trying them on and pretending to be on the stage, a dancer like her older cousin.

Aileen remembers that at one point in the late 1930s the whole family had to move to a large terraced house in the centre of town. She does not know why, but knew that they had to do it quickly and quietly and that Aileen was not to tell anyone. To this day the family never talked about the sudden move. However, Aileen loved the move as the house was much bigger than the previous one, it was also very close to the cinema, in the centre of Eastbourne.

She recalls that often on an evening when the cinema-goers were queuing up, waiting for the cinema to open, they would stand directly outside their front door and the line of people seemed to go on forever, right the way down the street and around the corner. Aileen and her younger brother Peter would sit in the front parlour window and stare at the people in the queue, knocking on the window and sticking their tongues out at them.

Another source of entertainment during this time was the Spiritualist Church just around the corner from the house. Aileen remembers her and her friends daring one another to go and knock on the door of the church when there was a service going on. However, on one occasion Aileen was caught red-handed by the people at the church and marched back to her mum. She remembers that she was given a severe telling off and was not allowed out for what seemed like weeks.

Aileen remembers her dad with great fondness and how much she adored him. He was kind and lovely and she often used to wonder how he and her very strict mother had met and got married. She recalled how her dad would like to drink. He worked on the railway and did a manual job and always came home filthy from his work. One thing that she didn't like though was how her mum would often send her to the public house on the corner of the road to go and see if he was in there, knowing that sending a small 8-year-old girl into the pub would make her dad follow her home to make sure she was all right. Aileen hated going into the pub, the smells of the beer and the fog of cigarette smoke which used to seep out of the saloon bar and then the worst part was having to go into the place and look for her dad. Most of the time she could find him and would run up to him and give him a huge hug, telling him that Mum wanted him home for dinner. Other times when she was not able to find him, he could not be found anywhere and those nights were awful as he would eventually come home when it was dark and Aileen and her brothers and sisters were all in bed. They would hear him stumble and stagger about on the floorboards and then hear their mum shouting at him, but she never heard him say anything back. Back then Aileen said she did not really understand about the drinking and the problems it caused, but growing up she learnt what her dad had experienced in the First World War and how difficult life must have been for him, every day. He had lost his brother in France along with many friends and that was something he would never get over, so the drinking was his way of blotting out the past.

She remembered that her mum and dad used to argue about something else also. Before they had married, dad had been married to another lady who died giving birth to a son. This would often cause a rift between the couple as the son was brought up by dad's older sisters as Aileen's mum had not wanted anything to do with him.

The 1950s also saw three-quarters of the population attending church at least once a week. It was during the 1950s that Eastbourne was referred to in many journals such as *Women's Weekly* and *Good Housekeeping*, at the time as education was the town's chief industry and very highly regarded. At this point there were several established schools such as Eastbourne College, which offered private education for both boys and girls, and children would attend these schools from other towns and cities. The town benefited from these schools due to the number of staff required to run them and provide an education in the vast array of subjects which were available to the students.

Mrs Eileen Dowd from Ipswich remembers attending a church in Eastbourne with her family when she was about 9 or 10 years old:

I remember every Sunday we had to be up early and have breakfast before getting ready in our best clothes to walk to church. I never really saw the point of this and I think it was more for Mum's benefit than anything else. Mum always wore her best clothes and a hat – clothes which I think she only used to wear to church. I never liked going to church as it was so boring and I was often told off by Mum for staring at the older ladies in their large hats and posh dresses, I would often wonder why they wore such pretty dresses just to sit in the cold church and that they should save them for when the weather was lovely and they could walk along the seafront.

We lived in a small house close to the railway station. My dad worked in an office to do with the railway and in the late 1950s we moved to Cambridge as I was told that dad had to do a more important job and so we left Eastbourne behind. I remember though walking to a church – again I am not that sure where it was in Eastbourne, but it seemed to take forever to get there and to get back and I remember that we even had to go even if it was raining hard. Mum used to say, 'a bit of rain won't do you any harm'. It was always so cold in the church too, even in the summer and no matter how I tried I always felt cold. Mum always told me that we had to go to church so that when we died we would go to heaven and I believed this. Although I have not been back to a church service since I was married in the 1970s.

Looking back, I don't think Mum and Dad were religious really, I think it was more to do with having to attend church regularly as everyone else we knew did and it would not be good to not be seen in the congregation. I also think that Mum liked to show off her latest new dress to some of the other ladies as I sometimes caught one or two of them looking Mum up and down in an envious way. But I never told her.

CHAPTER FOUR

Quality of Life

During the 100 years from 1850-1950, health and wealth went hand in hand, the better your status in society, the better your health was. Today, sadly we often take for granted the superb service which is offered by the National Health Service (NHS), however if we were to turn the clock back to pre-NHS, the population really would have had something to moan about. The Eastbourne area has had various institutions offering healthcare in several disciplines of medicine, including a specialist tuberculosis (TB) hospital which was located where the Crumbles Shopping complex currently stands in the harbour area. There were also convalescent homes and hotels offering the environment for the wealthier to come to Eastbourne for a period to recover from illness or disease, noting that the sea air offered positive effects for such patients.

In 1903, an asylum was built at Hellingly, East Sussex some 11 miles from the town to accommodate the growing number of patients who required psychiatric help, mainly as inpatients. It was designed with its own railway, mainly for transporting the vast amounts of coal needed to fuel the estate's boilers. It was built at a time when another hospital in Haywards Heath, West Sussex was overcrowded and so land was sought to create a new hospital. A 400-acre farm estate was acquired for this project at Hellingly and sadly the wards always seemed to be full. The hospital provided not only patients with a suitable environment, but also employed many doctors, nurses and other orderlies to run the hospital effectively. Hellingly would have touched the lives of many local women, whether they were patients at the house or worked there.

A lady who used to live in Hellingly as a young girl contacted me when she heard about my research. She does not want her name to be published. She described how, as a young girl, her family rented a cottage on the edge of the village of Hellingly, not that far from the hospital. She was often told by her parents not to go near the big house and never to talk to anyone that she saw wandering around the grounds, as they were probably unwell and should be left in peace. She recalled how one day, when she and her friends were playing in the lane near the hospital, they dared one another to go into the grounds of the house and stay there for as long as they could. She explained that there were always lots of stories going around about the hospital and the kind of patients they had there; mad people who killed children, or who had two heads and the like. Far-fetched and made up, most of the time, children could not help but be inquisitive.

The children were found messing about by one of the groundsmen and were escorted back home to their parents, who gave them a stern telling off and they were forbidden to set foot near the house again. A few years later, when their mother gave birth to baby number five and they outgrew their tiny cottage, they moved from Hellingly to a bigger house in Seaford.

It is easy to forget just how much medicine has changed over the centuries compared with what we have today. During the mid- to late nineteenth century, becoming ill and the fear of death and disease were at the forefront of everyone's mind, with the main obstacle to receiving care and the kind of treatment one received greatly dependent on wealth and class. The wealthy could call upon a doctor to attend to their every ache and pain, whereas the poor had to wait until they had no other alternative but to seek medical advice, by which time it was often too late. Many people at the time made use of home remedies, as the costs involved in having a doctor visit them was way above the kind of money they had access to and were able to afford. However, those who had a little spare money found so-called 'remedies' in the newspapers and publications of the time which offered a home postal service. Unfortunately, some of these potions were reported to cause more problems than they resolved.

A Children's Home was opened in the Holywell area of Eastbourne in 1891 and was a memorial to Harriet Brownlow Byron, who founded the All Saints Community of Sisters of the Poor. The home could accommodate up to 130 children at any one time.

Reforms to the Eastbourne Workhouse

Wilhelmina Brodie Hall (1845-1939)

Although little is known about this remarkable lady and what she did, she was fundamental in bringing about changes to so many children who had found themselves in a workhouse school. She grew up in Eastbourne where her father was a doctor. The family lived at Elm Cottage, South Street, which is now incorporated into Grove Road.

In taking an interest in the lives of local people, Wilhelmina became aware of the harsh conditions of Eastbourne workhouse. Even though food was commonly scarce, she discovered that pregnant women who had entered the workhouse were being deprived of food for up to nine days following the birth of their children. Committed to change, Wilhelmina was elected to the Board of Guardians in 1883.

Soon after, she set up a ladies committee dedicated to fostering children to ensure they would receive better care than the workhouse could provide in the accommodation that Wilhelmina reported to be very unsatisfactory. Her dedication to getting children to board out even led to some children being sent to Canada to be fostered.

St Mary's Hospital in Eastbourne was in Church Street and was previously known as the workhouse from 1817, when the Eastbourne Guardians established a workhouse at this location, renting premises that had been used as barracks during the Napoleonic Wars. The Eastbourne Poor Law Union was formed on 25 March 1835 and its operation was overseen by a Board of

Guardians who represented the numerous parishes in the area. At the time of the 1831 census the population which fell under the Union was 7,823. The Board of Guardians kept the workhouse for use by the Union and in 1859 finally purchased the site. The main building stood at the heart of the location with various other outbuildings, including converted stables and a chapel which dated from 1857. In 1877, an infectious diseases hospital was erected on the site and was later converted to an infirmary in 1887.

It was reported in the *Eastbourne Herald* in 1939 that a crowded audience attended and eagerly watched the demonstration given by the Eastbourne Women's League of Health and Beauty at the Winter Garden, the previous week. They demonstrated the heightened numbers of people falling victim to influenza and how a glass of Phosferine Tonic Wine was the safest and most pleasant way of warding it off. The speakers told ladies that the manufacturers would gladly forward them a free sample bottle on receipt of 3d in postage stamps to cover the cost of postage and packaging.

Public health

Public health was a concern in the late 1870s and towns and cities up and down the country held regular meetings to try and come to some sort of solution to the problems which arose. Some meetings did not always go as planned and there are notes from an Anti-Vaccination meeting which was organised in Eastbourne in 1877 to discuss the proposed compulsory vaccinations for children. It was stated that at the time only 35 per cent of the local population were against the action. A great deal of hostility was reported in various locations around the country following the suggestion of the vaccination scheme. Most of the medical profession at the time were in favour of the idea of vaccination as they could easily see the benefits as opposed to the risks associated with not getting the vaccination or the much-speculated side effects of the vaccine, especially for diseases such as smallpox. One speaker who presented in Eastbourne spoke of his recent visits to smallpox hospitals, the disease he felt was of the most impure.

The lecturer quoted statistics showing the number of deaths from smallpox in England in the epidemic of 1857-50 to be 14,244, in the years 1863-65 be 20,050 and in the epidemic of 1870-72 at 44,840. Taking into account the increase in population of 7 per cent between the first and second epidemic, the increase of smallpox in the same period had been 60 per cent. If increase in population between the second and third epidemic was 10 per cent, this meant the increase of deaths from smallpox during the same period was 120 per cent.

A report in the *Eastbourne Herald* quoted the following:

> *The humble Petition of the inhabitants of Eastbourne in public meeting, May 24th, 1877, felt that the vaccination was worthless and injurious and unjust to expect the population to be used in this way.*

Concerns were raised in Eastbourne in 1874 when a lady who travelled from outside of the town arrived at Eastbourne and had to be admitted to the hospital as she had contracted smallpox. There were queries as to whether the lady had contracted the disease whilst she has been in the workhouse. This case put the people and the medical profession of the town on high alert, due to the large number of visitors who came to Eastbourne each year. Fever wards were set up to isolate these patients, and were intended to provide care for people whatever their status, rich or poor, as the disease certainly did not choose its host. However, if the patient was able to pay for the treatment then they would be asked to do so.

Significant worry also arose in the late 1870s around the conditions of dwellings in Seaside and how easy it was for the spread of contagious diseases to take hold there, due to inadequate draining and sanitary systems for what was such a densely overcrowded area.

Another significant contributor to disease were the public lodging houses in Seaside which at times were overcrowded with a constant change of people from all over the place. Reports from residents in Leaf Terrace were of stagnant pools of water which built up on a regular basis in the Seaside area.

Concerns increased as the death rate from smallpox in Eastbourne grew. The town suffered greatly and authorities were starting to understand that it was not just the cities which fell foul to these virulent diseases. A great number of towns up and down the country suffered at the hands of smallpox. Smallpox was not the only major problem at the time; another disease which was spreading was typhoid fever. It was reported that there had never been such a desperate account of the state of public health previously issued by the authorities. However, quite extraordinarily, Eastbourne not only escaped from the clutches of the typhoid fever but in fact during the period the mortality rate reduced significantly.

CHAPTER FIVE

Social Life

At the start of the period covering this 100-year era, little could have been known of the changes that would take place with regards to how women could and would spend their leisure time and the recreational groups and pursuits that they would become involved in by the start of the 1950s.

During the Victorian period, ideas involving what women should do in the form of leisure and hobbies were practically unheard of and this continued in some extent right through this 100-year period. For the wealthy and middle classes, activities such as the arts, painting, drawing, maybe learning a new language could be arranged and this was usually in the woman's own home. The Victorian woman could take short walks only if accompanied as it was certainly not the done thing for a well-respected woman to be seen in public on her own. Sadly, there was little in the way of entertainment for women of Victorian Britain which seemed to offer any happiness.

By the time of the Edwardian period, people were far more liberal-minded in their thoughts and ideas. One area of Edwardian life where this was evident was the seaside experience. For many there was nothing like escaping to the coastal towns of Hastings and Eastbourne and partaking in an invigorating dip in the sea. Gone was Victorian prudishness as bathers were spared the blushes of the female bathers. Just a little way along the coast from Eastbourne is the sleepy town of Bexhill-on-Sea and it was here in 1901 that bathers of both sexes could mix on the beach for the first time. Beyond the attractions of the beach, the Edwardians realised that there was huge potential in these new towns, or 'resorts' as they became known, and they grew into the coastline industry we know today.

One element of the Edwardian seaside experience which stood out more than anything else was the pier. Many of these started off life as a means for getting people off the steamer boats to the shore, however they steadily grew in stature. There was everything on the Edwardian pier from kiosks and theatres to side shows and amusement arcades. You entered through a turnstile paying a nominal fee and what opened before you was a world of brightly coloured wrought iron in beautiful decorative detailing, balconies and benches. Everything about the pier leant towards the exotic and escapism, with designs in oriental themes, domed roofs and mythical sea creatures, with mermaids adorning the decoration. One major attraction on a pier was the fortune teller, who attracted hundreds of eager customers each day – many of them being young single women wishing to know when they would get married. This was a very popular attraction and was found on most piers up and down the country including Eastbourne and Hastings. Eastbourne pier has always attracted visitors to its genteel Victorian splendour and has offered what is so uniquely British to all its visitors. The pier's history began in April 1865.

Eastbourne Pier has an interesting story, touching the hearts of many people who visit each year. The pier was created by the Eastbourne Pier Company in 1866 who raised a working fund of £15,000 and was opened in 1870 by Lord E. Cavendish although at this stage it was not fully completed and wasn't until 1872. Eastbourne pier followed a design which is seen in many other seaside towns in England built around the same time when the health benefits of 'holidaying' by the sea were being recognised and these places were also becoming fashionable. The design of the pier is that it is 300 metres long and constructed on stilts which rest in supports on the seabed which allow for movement during bad weather.

The entrance you see today is not how the original was designed, originally you would enter the pier by the lower promenade, but due to the severe storms and bad weather which hit the coast in 1877, the structure was badly damaged and swept into the sea and therefore the pier entrance was rebuilt in an elevated position.

In 1888, the pier saw the construction of a domed area which could house 400 seats and was replaced two years later by a 1,000-seat theatre, bar, camera obscura and saloons thus offering the visitor a whole new experience by the sea.

During World War Two, the pier had a new a type of visitor in the form of machine guns which made the pier their home as this was the perfect location to watch for enemy invasions. Sadly in 1942 a mine exploded causing considerable damage to the pier and the surrounding area.

In 2014, a fire took hold of part of the beautiful old building causing significant damage. It underwent extensive reconstruction to bring it back to life and continues to charm locals and visitors to this seaside town today.

Much of the disorganised entertainment of the seaside towns was brought under control in the Edwardian period, when licences were awarded to establishments such as theatres and music halls, and acts were in set venues forming more of a structure to the seaside economy. The Edwardian period's legacy to seaside towns was the grand ornate hotels, beautiful pavilions, piers and promenades which have continued to attract visitors to them to this day. Many of this can still be seen in Eastbourne today, including many of the grand and elegant hotels located on the seafront.

Tennis Tournaments at Devonshire Park

One sport which has always been linked to Eastbourne is that of the game of tennis, played at Devonshire Park, and the first tennis tournament was held here in August 1881 for women only. Women's singles tournaments gained popularity in the 1880s and it was well-known as the season-ending event at the South of England Championships each September.

Some of the ladies who were involved included Dorothea Chambers, Blanche Hillyard and Charlotte Sterry. Dorothy Lambert Chambers was a British tennis player who won several tournaments at Wimbledon and a gold medal at the Olympics in 1908. Blanche Hillyard was another remarkable tennis player who completed in the first ever Wimbledon championships in 1884 and Charlotte Cooper Sterry won titles at both Wimbledon and the Olympics in 1900. In 1922, Irene Ryan, a citizen from South Africa, took the crown in Eastbourne.

One lady was instrumental in making a difference to the lives of many girls and women: **Emily Mary Shackleton (nee Dorman).** Emily Mary Dorman, who would later become known as Lady Emily Shackleton, was born in 1868 into a large wealthy family in Kent. Her surname is best known for her husband's Arctic explorations. Through the contacts Emily had, she could fill the time when her husband was away with activities with her children, combined with becoming the Eastbourne Divisional Commissioner for the Girl Guides. She met Ernest Shackleton, who was six years her junior, and Ernest was besotted with Emily. However, he was a dreamer and had great plans which often did not include his wife. Whilst her husband was away on his long expeditions, there was no communication between them, leaving Emily to become very self-sufficient. This pattern was a normal way of life for the couple for much of their married life. Sadly, during his final expedition Ernest died and he left his family with a significant amount of debt as he had never been good with finances or business matters.

The First World War was the catalyst that made Emily Shackleton who she was – as it was for many other women at that time. She took on roles that she would never have before and even opened a bazaar in aid of the Red Cross. Around this time the family moved to Eastbourne and it was here that Emily became involved in the Girl Guides eventually becoming the divisional commissioner for Eastbourne. She also took up playing golf in Eastbourne, a pastime which she greatly enjoyed and something she would never have done if her husband had been at home. When Ernest the great explorer came home in

1909 there would have been many engagements that he would have taken part in as everyone wanted to hear about the places he had been and his experiences. People wanted to know Ernest Shackleton as he was somewhat of a celebrity of the day. He had set a new world record and was knighted by King Edward VII. He gained a lot of female attention and admirers and this often caused a level of conflict between Emily and Ernest.

Emily died in 1936, following a long illness. At a time when it was not considered the done thing for a married lady to work, Emily proved that this was indeed a positive action for women and instead of becoming a home maker she stepped out and took on new roles. She kept herself constantly busy during the war years, helping out when and where she could and became part of a strong network of women. Emily's story highlights the struggles she faced coming from a wealthy and supportive family to marrying and feeling very much alone in a relationship. She was strong enough to form new bonds with other women and by setting up the local Girl Guides' group, she could empower young women for future generations.

Being a professional musician has never been an easy career for women and the fierce world of 1880's England was no exception for one such talented young lady by the name of Violet Gordon-Woodhouse.

Violet Gordon-Woodhouse was born on 23 April 1871 to James Gwynne and Mary Earle. She grew up during her early years in the village of Folkington, just outside of Eastbourne – the family home was the manor house in the village – and the rest of her time was spent at the family's house in Harley Street, London. As a young child, Violet's talent for music was apparent and she soon became known as a specialist in Elizabethan music, playing the harpsichord. She spent much of her young life surrounded by musicians and was frequently taken to concerts and the opera by her mother. Violet was tutored on the piano by her mother and attended her first audition at the age of 7 years old. From a young age Violet wanted to become a professional musician, however her father would not allow this as he considered it beneath the family's position in society if she were to perform publicly as an unmarried woman. In 1893 a suitable match was found, but no marriage took place as the relationship did not blossom. Shortly after this Violet was introduced to Gordon Woodhouse, a friend of her brother, and they married in July 1895. This marriage was not conventional; for Violet, it was a way of enabling her to indulge in her musical passion without the scorn of her father.

Violet was recognised as one of the greatest keyboard players of her time and her career up until the First World War was successful. After the war, however, her father died, leaving Violet poor as she had recently left her husband and so had no means of support. She decided that she needed to find the help of an agent and turned to Ibbs and Tillett who booked her to play in private homes.

In 1920, Violet was noted as being the first person to be recorded playing the harpsichord and successfully signed a contract with a gramophone company for the next few years.

The Grand Hotel became the place to visit for anyone spending time in Eastbourne and very much a place to be seen. The hotel offered everything for the luxury-end guest, including private bathrooms, which were the new thing; it was no longer considered good enough to have communal bathrooms and maids bringing hot water to the room – this belonged in the past. In the mid-1920s the hotel completed renovation work and each room was fitted with its own bathroom facility. Wealthy and famous guests continued to stay at The Grand including Jim Mollison, MBE who broke world records in the world of aviation, and his wife Amy Johnson who was the first women to fly alone from London to Australia.

A Mrs Westwood wrote a short account of how she remembers that she and another girl who worked as chambermaids between 1926 and 1928 got into a fight in one of the staff dormitories over one of the waiters. Mrs Westwood told the other girl that she could have him – but Mrs Westwood was the one who ended up marrying him. Mrs Westwood also remembers being chosen with one of the other girls who worked in the laundry to sell cotton wool snowballs at a charity ball. She wore high-legged boots, a short white skirt and a silk top hat.

One iconic building in Eastbourne which has long been a highlight on the social calendar and visited by thousands each year is Eastbourne Pier and an interesting article from the *Eastbourne Gazette* in 1898, described an act in the Pier Ballroom:

> *THE PIER PAVILION. Patrons of the Pier Pavilion may be interested to know that Miss Maria Dalroyde, the Eastbourne actress who recently earns a fortune, is appearing at this place of amusement during the present week as a member of Mr. Edward Neville's variety company. The entertainment consists of several miscellaneous turns. Mr. Edward Neville keeps the entertainment going a brisk rate, and builds on the fine reputation he built on during the winter months.*

Another lady of note from Eastbourne for this period was Florence Amelia Hutchinson. While many women practised photography in their spare time, seldom did any of them develop their interest and passion into a business. Florence went against the tradition of this male-dominated business and branched out on her own, often publishing her work anonymously or with just her initials so that no one would be put off by her gender.

She quickly established herself as a creator of high quality images of Sussex and produced many wonderful cards depicting the county. She produced sets of cards of Hampden Park in Eastbourne and the Downland area around Eastbourne which were highly popular. She was also involved in taking the annual photographs of sports clubs and groups around the area. Florence continued working into the 1930s.

In 1935, a bandstand designed in a 'Neo-Grec' style by Leslie Rosevere was installed on Eastbourne seafront. Today it has become one of the landmarks of the town and a very popular entertainment venue. Originally it was designed to seat 3,500 people, however this was reduced to more comfortably seat 1,500. The original structure dated back to 1866. It has been featured in TV's *Foyles War* drama and offers inspiration to artists and photographers the world over. Today, bands play and shows are performed here year-round, and the location offers a different venue against the backdrop of the sea. At the rear of the auditorium there is a plaque and this commemorates the Eastbourne Bandsman John Woodward, who was one of those playing in the band on the Titanic on that fateful day of 15 April 1912.

A Miss Powell contacted me to share some memories that her grandmother had told her about visiting the bandstand in the late 1930s, not long after it had opened. Her grandmother described how she and her best friend visited a few concerts at the open-air bandstand as it really was a place to be seen in Eastbourne. You would dress up in your best clothes and hat and walk along the promenade first before taking your seat. Some nights the area was packed as the seats were quite cheaply priced – although you could not always rely on what the weather would do and it was always recommended that you wrap up warm on an evening.

Another location which was popular during the mid-1930s for young people to visit was the Winter Garden, especially when a dance was being held. During the war years there were often tea dances held as this attracted many local ladies and an equal if not greater number of soldiers who were posted in Eastbourne.

A lady got in touch with me who used to live in Eastbourne, a Mrs Cynthia Young, who told me that if it hadn't been for the war then her parents would never have met. Her mum met a very nice, handsome soldier at one of the tea dances who asked Cynthia's mum if she would like to dance. Well, she accepted the offer but never thought that she would end up marrying the young man. Cynthia explained that her mum and her friends were regulars at the tea dances held at the Winter Garden and that she had had her eye on this young man for a few weeks, he turned out to be called Harry Vernon, and the rest is history. They were engaged shortly after they met and married at the end of the war.

Eastbourne was well supplied with cinemas, with a total of nine. The advent of talking pictures meant big investments were needed by the cinema owners to be able to supply films with sound, but it was the way that cinema was going and what people expected and by 1930, all of Eastbourne's cinemas had been wired for sound. A night at the cinema was a big night out for people and many looked forward all week to seeing their favourite stars of the screen.

Monday, 3 April 1933 saw a carnival extravaganza to mark the opening of the Luxor Cinema in Pevensey Road, Eastbourne. The Luxor was very prestigious with a Compton organ in the theatre together with illuminated lights set around the organ display. Compton organs were made by John Compton especially for cinemas and were the most prevalent organs in the UK, with some 261 in UK theatres alone. Compton also designed and built organs for many churches. Messages were received on the opening night from film stars of the day wishing the Luxor the very best of luck. The Luxor really was the height of luxury and quite unlike any other cinema in the town. Beautiful curtains were hung around the stage and recorded sound was provided at all presentations. All the furnishings in the foyer were provided by Bobby and Co. ('Bobby's' – 1887–1972), a chain of high-end department stores found in various seaside towns around the country. They were known for selling luxury brands and offering 'the magic of shopping' to the customer. The buildings were usually very ornate with sumptuous interior design. 'Bobby's' Eastbourne is now where Debenham's stands on Terminus Road.

The Luxor was also fitted with an automatic ticket machine which offered the customers speed and efficiency in purchasing their tickets, this was the first of its kind in Eastbourne. The cinema even had illuminated ashtrays in every part of the building. When the cinema opened there was an officially appointed hairdresser to give all their usherettes the glamorous uniform blonde hair-dos, like many of the stars of the day.

Mrs Natalie Wood, who now lives in Seaford, contacted me with a little snippet about her grandmother, Mrs Sarah Walton (née Stockbridge) who, at the age of 19, applied to be an usherette at The Luxor. It was considered a very well-respected position and the perks like the uniform and having your very own hairdresser appealed to the young Sarah very much. She remembers hearing about the jobs and she was required to attend an interview on a certain day and time. What she didn't know was that it would be a group interview. However, as Sarah arrived at The Luxor she was turned away almost straight away being told that her hairstyle was not suitable and neither was it the right colour for their usherettes. Natalie remembers her mum talking about this and how upset Sarah had been at not being given a chance to pursue her dream job.

Not only did The Luxor show film presentations, it was also a venue for live bands, which were extremely popular in the thirties and mainly showcased on a Sunday night. Such bands as 'Jack Hylton and His Boys' and 'Debroy Somers and His Band' drew the crowds in.

1932 saw a local Eastbourne lady bowler successfully beating the current singles bowls champion. The title was held by Mrs Tigg from Croydon who was defeated by Ms Devall of the Redoubt Bowls Club, Eastbourne. Eastbourne was the first town in England to hold a bowling tournament which was exclusively for women. Women travelled from all over the country to compete in this competition, which was a great success.

CHAPTER SIX

Political Life

The National Union of Women's Suffrage Societies (NUWSS) was led by Millicent Fawcett and was formed in 1897. The group was formed of mainly middle-class women who campaigned in a peaceful way. They slowly and steadily gained the support of Parliament, working towards private members' bills to give women the vote.

The Women's Social and Political Union (WSPU) was formed in 1903 and led by Emmeline Pankhurst. This group was also middle-class, however they had a different approach to that of the NUWSS. They openly heckled politicians, held marches, chained themselves to railings, attacked policemen, set fire to buildings and went on active hunger strikes to name but a few of their highly powerful activities. It was one of their members, Emily Davison, who ran out in front of the king's horse on Derby day, 1913, and was killed.

For working-class women there was the East London Federation of Suffragettes. Formed by Sylvia Pankhurst in 1914, they believed in social reform and were against the violence of the WSPU.

It was during February 1918 the Representation of the People Act finally gave women over the age of 30 (who were married or owned property) the vote and in 1928 this was extended to all women over the age of 21.

Up and down the country the argument had been the same, wherever meetings were held. Some of the commonly voiced opinions heard were:

- A woman's place was in the home and going out into the rough world of politics would change her caring nature. The argument against this was that women are equal before God, and therefore should have the vote.
- It was stated by many men that women should not be allowed the vote as they did not fight in wars. However, this was responded to by the many women who paid taxes at the time.
- Many firmly believed that women were too ignorant of politics to be able to use their vote properly. This angered many women who were doctors and mayors and did a far better role than their male contenders.
- Also, it was believed that if women were given the vote, this would mean Parliament would be ruined by the likes of the violent Suffragettes – however, as had been seen in other countries, where women had received the vote, this was not the case at all.

Suffragette Activity in Eastbourne

There are numerous interesting accounts of suffragette activity in Eastbourne and a few have been selected from the newspapers at the time to highlight the plight suffered and the achievements of many. Until I started researching this area of work I had no idea of the incredible work achieved by women connected to Eastbourne and the difficulties they encountered along the way without giving up. They are inspiring to say the least.

In a copy of the *Eastbourne Gazette* of 1 July 1914, there is a report concerning the Eastbourne suffragettes' hunger strike. The strike lasted for eight days, with the women drinking no water for three days:

EIGHT DAYS WITHOUT FOOD. Eastbourne Suffragettes' Hunger Strike. NO WATER FOR THREE DAYS. REVELATIONS OF PRISON LIFE. Two of the suffragettes who participated in the recent attempt—headed by Mrs. Pankhurst—to present a petition to His Majesty the King but for family reasons they do not wish their names to published. In order to distinguish the one from the other will refer to them as Mrs. A and Miss B. Both witnessed the scenes which wrought them up to such a pitch of indignation that they determined to be arrested; and they were incarcerated in Holloway Gaol where they continued the hunger strike they had begun in the police station. On the fifth day Miss B was released. Her less fortunate companion (Mrs. A) was eight days in prison and was finally released in a terribly enfeebled condition. Throughout her detention she did not eat a particle of solid food; but she was unable to maintain the thirst-strike for more than three days. As she had been suffering from chronic appendicitis, she was the last person who should have entered upon such an adventure—from the point of view of worldly wisdom. But she is an enthusiast regarding the cause; and she asserts that imprisonment, so far from crushing the spirit of the suffragettes, confirms them in their militancy. On Thursday last a representative of the Eastbourne Gazette *endeavoured to see her, but was informed that she was suffering from a heart attack and needed complete rest. He was able, however, to obtain an interview with her on Friday evening when she gave a very clear account of her trying experiences.*

THE EFFECT OF A SEVERE BLOW.

A mounted constable tried to force his horse against me, but was unsuccessful. I happen to know something about horses, and turned the animal aside. Then he called the men on foot to his assistance, and our little group was broken up. The police would not arrest us, but would not let us proceed along the road. They lifted us up and put us over the low railings among the crowd. One was wearing new pair of gloves, and one of the fingers caught the edge of a policeman's stripes. Possibly he thought I was going to tear off his stripes, but I had no such intention. Suddenly he struck me a violent blow just below my right collar-bone, the effect caused a serious swelling. The moment I felt as if my collar-bone had been broken, and my right arm seemed paralysed. The police were so numerous that for nearly two hours they tried in vain to break through the cordon. Finding it impossible, and seeing that the police were determined handle us roughly, but on no account to arrest us, they gave up the attempt and went to have some tea.

MRS. A's NARRATIVE. THE PANKHURST PROCESSION TOWARDS THE PALACE.

When we had recovered we began to discuss the dreadful scenes we had witnessed that afternoon. There were dozens of women who had received far rougher treatment than we had experienced. Some had their clothes torn; others had bleeding faces; and some had been dragged along in a collapsed state by the policemen. None but eye-witnesses could credit the exhibition of savagery on the part of the police which took place within a stone's throw of the palace of the King. As an old member of the W.S.P.U. One sent in name to serve on Mrs Pankhurst's deputation to present our petition to the King. In Grosvenor Square we formed up in procession of about 230. Many women fell in afterwards. I was within two or three yards of Mrs. Pankhurst at the start, as I was in the third rank.

We made our way towards the Wellington Arch, where many police, some on foot and some mounted, seemed to lay waiting for us. We made an immediate rush for the gates which, although closed, were not locked. The rush was dreadful, and the horses were made to move among the women, agonising shrieks being heard from those who were thrown to the ground.

My companion and I tried to keep together, and owing to our position we were the first to get through the gate. I had no sooner passed through than a bulky policeman, without any warning, threw me down at full length on to the pavement. If a gentleman had not partly caught me, my head would have been smashed against the bottom of the gate.

Stunned, and almost unable for the moment to realise what had happened, I turned my head and saw a young girl lying near me with her mouth and teeth covered with blood. Amid a general cry of "Get up!" I rose with the help of some bystanders. I jumped up quickly as I suddenly realized that other women coming through would be piled on top of me.

A further report from the *Eastbourne Gazette*, 8 July 1914 continues the story:

HUNGER-STRIKE   IN   PRISON.   Eastbourne Suffragettes' Experiences. EIGHT DAYS WITHOUT FOOD.

[In our last issue we published the first portion of an account of the experiences of two suffragettes who were arrested in London and sentenced to a term of imprisonment in Holloway Gaol on a charge of breaking a window. Miss B was released after five days' detention. Mrs. A was imprisoned for eight days; and subjoin the second and concluding portion narrative.]

WHY WAS MISS B RELEASED?

The next day my friend who had been sentenced with me was released. She had been told that she would be released the previous evening, and under those circumstances she had taken some milk. She was in much better health than myself, and I have never been able to understand why she was treated differently. This was on the Wednesday, the sixth day after our arrest.

I had now become absolutely indifferent whether they released me or not. My friend was going to give the news to my husband, and that relieved me a great deal. I shouted to her through the wall that on no account must my fine be paid. It was afternoon before my friend was allowed to go, for she had been ready since six o'clock in the morning.

There was lot of going to and fro from to her cell on the part of the officials, and they kept on altering the time of departure so that she began to doubt whether she was really going to be let out or not.

I must point out that we had adjoining cells, but the walls were so thick that it was very difficult to converse with my comrade, and I did not try to do so after Wednesday.

When at last my friend left I felt so pleased that it made me forget my own troubles.

NO NIGHT CLOTHES PROVIDED – SUFFERING FROM COLD

I had no night clothes to sleep in, and was refused a bath when I asked for one, the reason being that I had declined to eat. Owing to the cold I had to keep on my boots when I was in bed.

On the Thursday morning I tried get up to wash myself, but I fell down in a heap and had to creep back into bed. I had no pain but I felt so cold that my teeth chattered and I was shaking all over for some time.

The wardress came in and brought me a hot-water bottle and asked if I wanted to see the doctor. I said "No!" but he came all the same. He asked me if I would take some Brand's essence of beef, and when I refused he said it was very foolish, for I would suffer for it later in life and that I was undermining my constitution, and that he could not see the use of it himself.

Although speaking had become a very hard task, I managed to say what he had doubtless heard many times before. I said I was fighting for a principle and that I did not intend give in. If they wanted my life they could have it. "Why (I asked him) was I treated differently from my friend, who had been released?" We were sentenced for the same offence. Did he not think that I had been punished sufficiently for my offence?

Then I was overcome and unable to say more. The doctor replied that it had to do with the Secretary of State and left my cell.

A STRANGE EXPERIENCE.

I heard that we could have lemon and hot water, so I asked the wardress for some and she brought it at once. I thought lemon would take away the nasty thickness in my mouth. I had only swallowed a mouthful when a most extraordinary thing happened. My mouth became full was if with food and I could not swallow. Getting short of breath, I put my fingers into my mouth to get it out.

It was the skin of my tongue, palate, gums and throat, which seemed have detached itself from the flesh. I kept on tearing it away as fast as I could. Some of the pieces were inches in length and there seemed to be no end to them.

I became so alarmed and my whole body was shaking that tried to get up to ring the bell. I did not remember anything more till I awoke from a deep sleep, and it took me several minutes to realize where I was. I felt something in my mouth. It was some more skin, and that brought everything back to my mind.

I felt dreadfully thirsty, and on getting hold the cup on the chair near the bed it felt still warm, so I could not have been sleeping long after I collapsed. I was afraid to drink the lemon water and there was no other water.

I did not dare to try to get up again. So I waited for some time till I could not stand the burning thirst any longer, and took another sip of the lemon-water. It was most refreshing this time, and I did not take long to drink it all.

I heard the keys in the lock and once more they took away the food which had been placed near the door for my supper, and the door was locked for the night.

I was now almost feeling more comfortable than I had yet felt since entering Holloway. My head was clear and the happenings of the last week stood out clearly in my mind— the dreadful injustices I had seen towards others as well towards myself; the prison with all its gruesome methods and barbarities; and the cries of the women undergoing forcible feeding.

One of the unfortunate girls used to come in to clean the cells, and on being asked by myself what her offence was, told me that she had do a month for soliciting. The crushing treatment these girls received from the wardresses was shameful and cruel. I kept thinking whether it was possible that these conditions could go on. What were the people outside those walls thinking about the matter? It then occurred to me that they did not know. Only a week ago I was one of those who did not know. Then, at that very moment, I realized my reward for all my suffering in the knowledge that had come to me; and could I now retrace the step I had taken? It would be a shame indeed now that my eyes had been opened through my own suffering. Now I knew the need for this fight as only those who have gone through the experience of prison can know. Was I going to be crushed by this hand of tyranny? My body might be crushed, perhaps, but only when life itself shall have ceased will I give up the fight for this cause.

UNABLE TO STAND UP—RELEASED AT LAST

On the eighth day of my imprisonment (Thursday), I was unable to stand up when the doctor came. Even then he did not tell me he would release me. He felt my pulse. Then he went out of the cell.

I heard them snap the card from outside the cell door, and I suspected that that meant liberation. Soon after I was asked by the wardress where I would go if I were let out.

The doctor sent three wardresses to help dress me. I was carried out in a chair; they put me in a taxicab, and a wardress took me to a nursing home. On my arrival there they gave me a little milk and brandy and fed me on the principle of "a little and often." I stayed in the nursing home from the Friday till the following Tuesday; and I then returned to Eastbourne, a friend having kindly offered to accompany me to the station and see me safely into the train.

Marie Corbett (1859–1932)

Marie Corbett, born 30 April 1859, in Kennington, London, to parents George and Eliza from Tunbridge Wells. Marie was known as being a co-founder of the Liberal Woman's Suffrage Society. She came from a well-to-do middle-class family and was taught at home by several elderly, very strict ladies. Marie's parents involved her in political activism and this became a large part of her life as she was passionate about supporting votes for women and organising campaigns on the subject.

There was a constant dark cloud hanging over the poor of Victorian England, especially for women who had few rights and certainly no voice in politics. It was clear to some women that their place should be in the home, unless they were extremely wealthy and brave enough to break down the barriers that had been in place to quash their freedom and rights. However, Marie was one such women who overcame the stereotypical ideas and opinions of the time. She was a strong individual who wanted what was right and fought for what she whole-heartedly believed in. To the upper classes of Victorian society, the poor were mostly invisible, something which Marie had very strong feelings about. As a result, she fought and stood up against these beliefs and began her humanitarian career by trying to change the plight of the poor and the living conditions of the poorest children in society.

Victorian England was in the grip of an industrial revolution and many of the people who had worked in agriculture were now being discarded. Many of these land workers left the rural life they had grown used to and ventured to the towns and cities in search of work and a better life. However, this resulted in much overcrowding and unsanitary living conditions for thousands and by the end of the 1880s, it is estimated that one third of the population were living in poverty.

The Union Workhouse was introduced after the Poor Law Amendment Act was passed in 1834 to provide some support for the poor, elderly and ill. This was seen as a brilliant solution to the cascading poverty as it created a place for the poor and destitute to live and work. However, the Government feared that the new workhouse would make many people idle and would attract more than it helped, and so the conditions would be so harsh that no one would want to go there – or at least that was the plan. Despite this the workhouse saw increased numbers through its doors, and one fear which was prevalent to all who entered the workhouse was whether they would ever leave.

Men, women and children were segregated, dividing families and tearing them apart. It wasn't until 1891 that the Society for the Prevention of Cruelty to Children was formed, some sixty-seven years following the formation of The Society for the Prevention of Cruelty to Animals. In 1894, the Local Government Act enabled Marie to join as a member of the rural district council, following which members could become Poor Law Guardians, resulting in her standing and being elected to Uckfield Union Board of Guardians. Marie was also one of the first women in the county to become a councillor.

Marie further went on to carry out much humanitarian work in East Sussex and the Weald, which included finding people in communities who were open to fostering children. She extended this to Eastbourne and moved all the children in the workhouse to foster families who received 5 shillings per week to help with their keep. Marie visited these children each month and changed the lives of so many for the good. She would travel several miles to visit the workhouse and meet with the inmates there.

Marie married Charles Henry Corbett in 1880, and both supported one another and were devoted to the other's beliefs and ideas for some fifty years. Marie died at the age of 72 in 1932, having been instrumental in changing the lives of so many, sharing in a positive outlook.

What a remarkable lady who strove to make changes against the odds.

Meeting between the Eastbourne House of Commons and Mr Ashby from the Liberal Party

The following was shared with me by Mr Edward Thomas, who has carried out extensive research on the opening of the Hippodrome Theatre, Seaside in Eastbourne in 1883. The following is a report of the meeting held on 1 October 1883 and provides an interesting insight into the discussions and views of the time.

On 1 October 1883, the Eastbourne House of Commons met with Mr Ashby from the Liberal Party [who] rose to move the following resolution:

> *That in the opinion of the house The Parliamentary Franchise should be extended to women who possess the qualifications which entitles them to vote and who in all matters of local government, have a right of voting.*

Mr Ashby could not see how women who paid their fair share of taxes and were considered qualified to vote in municipal matters, and to sit on school boards and Boards of Guardians, should not be capable of voting for members of Parliament. Owing to the great extension of education, he saw no reason why female as well as male suffrage should not be the law of the land. The resolution was seconded.

The following are some of the responses received:

Mr Goldsmith, Conservatives

> *As a rule, women take little or no interest in political matters, and there is no reason why they should have more liberty given. As it is ladies have plenty of liberty at present. The real duty of women is in their homes, attending to*

domestic affairs, and not in the troubled area of politics, where they are quite out of place.

Going back to the origin of humans, man was given more vigour of mind, strength of body and force of character. It was man who hunted the game and toiled in the fields. To women was given another sphere, not less useful and worthy. To women essentially belonged the milder virtues, and in her sphere, she should rest contented, and not to seek to encroach upon the domain of man. The cry for female suffrage is only raised by a few strong-minded women. No true woman ever desires to enter competition with men.

This was received with cheers.

Mr Hillman objected to the bill because he did not feel that the ladies were sufficiently educated to receive the franchise. He explained that he used the word 'educate' in the political sense.

Very many ladies would be influenced by personal appearance of the candidates. A young and handsome fellow with a long, silken moustache and a sweet smile, but without brains or any knowledge of politics would have a far better chance of success than an old gentleman with a plain face and corpulent form, but who nevertheless was a good and sound speaker. The question of income tax or the relation of the government with foreign powers would never enter their dear little minds. The most wicked blue eyes and longest silkiest moustache would win the day.

Mr Edgeworth for the Liberals said that one reason for his opposing the motion was that in every 99 cases out of 100, even if women were given the franchise they would never use it. In many parts of the United Kingdom, elections were accompanied by turmoil and disturbance, which rendered it unpleasant even for men to vote, and it would be worse still for ladies. He thought on such days that the best place for women was in the home. He believed that as a rule, women did not trouble their heads about politics. In most instances, the ladies' vote would be influenced by their favourite doctors, lawyers or even curates. There might be some ladies who studied politics, but the greater majority of them thought more about their husbands' dinners and other comforts. That was more their sphere.

Mr Morrison, Conservative, thought that those gentleman in favour of the motion, could not have sufficient experience of women. No man could speak of women properly until he possessed that great blessing – a mother-in-law.

After the roars of laughter had died down, he went on to observe that when women joined the army and navy, joined the police, or when they went in for all the hard work and did the same as man, then they ought to be entitled to vote. At present he thought that their motto ought to be: 'Women for Women's Work'. He contended that the cry for women's suffrage was got up by the agitators.

In one of the lone voices of the night, Mr Ferrier for the Conservatives, supported the motion and said:

> Ladies are trying hard to emancipate themselves. They are gradually fighting the battle and in the end, will win the victory. Step by step they are advancing and in that victory which will come, I think they will have the best wishes of the opposite sex. Women are superior to men in many instances and there have been great women in the world whose example commands respect. I believe they would greatly add to the dignity of the country were they to be admitted to the suffrage.

The motion on being put forward was declared by the Deputy Speaker to be lost, the noes being greatly in the majority.

In 1897, the same year as the formation of the National Union of Women's Suffrage Societies, one of the most famous women of her time visited the New Theatre Royal in Eastbourne on 26 August. The lady in question was Dame Ellen Terry, the legendary actress.

Ellen visited Eastbourne to see her daughter Edith (Edy) Craig perform. Edy, like her mother, was immersed in the world of the theatre. She directed many plays, including several on women's rights and said that:

> *Plays have done such a lot for the Suffrage [Movement].*
> *They get hold of nice, frivolous people who would die sooner*
> *than go in cold blood to meetings. But they watch plays, and*
> *get interested, and then we can rope them in for meetings.*

The International Suffrage Bookshop was co-founded by Edith and she also sold the Votes for Women newspaper on the streets of London.

Edith's partner was Christabel Marshall, who wrote plays under the pseudonym Christopher St. John including one entitled *How the Vote Was Won*. She joined a march to the House of Commons in 1909 and was arrested for setting fire to a post box.

In a quiet residential area of Eastbourne known as Upperton you will find St Anne's Church in Upperton Gardens, a short distance north from the railway station. This often-overlooked church holds a secret. If you venture inside, in the Lady Chapel you will find a brass plaque to Captain Thomas Oates, a member of Captain Scott's Antarctic Expedition, who, when suffering from frostbite and exhaustion, walked out to his death in the snow rather than being a burden to his fellow men. Captain Oates was a worshipper at this church, and a painting close by the Oates memorial bears the marks of the militant suffragists, who scratched upon it 'Votes, Votes, Votes' and set fire to the church in 1913. Many of the activists and campaigners were reported to have caused damage to buildings and disrupted council meetings, and this is just one example.

Madam Mayor

An interesting article in the letters section of the *Croydon Advertiser* from 1939 read:

> *Sir – a few weeks ago I wrote some notes on the style*
> *and title of a lady who has been elected mayor of a*

borough, and pointed out that the customary address was Mr. Mayor. A correspondent has taken me to task on the matter and suggests that the best style of address is Madam Mayor. There appears to be no definite ruling on the point and what is customary is the only guidance we can look for in the matter. Some three or four years ago Eastbourne elected a lady mayor, and in order that the proper style of address should be adopted, careful inquiry was made. It was found that the address Mr. Mayor was in conformity with general practice. Consulting the Mayor this does not rule out the suggested address of Madam Mayor.

An article in the *Portsmouth Evening News* of 1926 describes Eastbourne's First Lady Mayor:

Eastbourne's First Lady Mayor.

Great public interest was had at Eastbourne during the ceremony of electing Councillor Miss Hudson, J.P., Mayor, she is the first woman to fill the position since the borough was incorporated 43 years ago. The Mayor said that although the honour had been directly conferred on her, she was also keen that she not only shared this with three other female colleagues, but with the women of the town generally.

The Story of Elsie Bowerman (1889–1973)

Elsie was born in Tunbridge Wells to William and Edith. Her father William was a successful draper who dealt in property investments. These investments meant that Elsie and her mother could live comfortably when William passed away when she was aged just 5.

At the age of 22, Elsie boarded the RMS *Titanic* in Southampton with her mother. When it hit an iceberg two days later, they managed to board one of the first lifeboats due to their status as both women and first class passengers.

She studied extensively at the Middle Temple in 1921 and was called to the Bar in 1924. She then went on to have a successful broadcasting career for the BBC.

Elsie led a remarkable life and made significant changes and advancements for women. As a member of the suffragette movement she attended marches, protests and took part in campaigns.

During the time she was at Girton College, Cambridge, there were several societies that Elsie was involved in. These were:

- 1920–1929 Honorary Secretary and Joint Founder of the Women's Guild of the Internationale.
- Member of the Council of Wycombe Abbey School.
- Director of Norland Nursery Training College.
- Honorary Secretary of the Union of Girls' Schools for Social Service.

As a campaigning suffragette, Elsie joined the Women's Social and Political Union (WSPU), started by Emmeline Pankhurst, becoming involved in increasingly more militant methods, such as interrupting political meetings; holding marches and demonstrations. Many women were injured and arrested, including Elsie's own mother Edith, who managed to escape unhurt from the infamous 'Black Friday' deputation. Elsie died at the age of 83 at Princess Alice Hospital, Eastbourne, from a stroke. At her funeral the Reverend Brown commented on her academic achievements in his eulogy: 'This was surely evidence of her determination to do the best she could and use her gifts for the benefit of her own sex. She was determined that women should have equal opportunities with men and for a time assisted Mrs Pankhurst in the Votes for Women campaign.'

Eastbourne Conservative Association

In 1939, the Meads Women's Branch of the Eastbourne Conservative Association was created to the excitement of many local women. The following was reported from the meeting of the branch. Councillor Miss Kenyon Stow was a guest speaker at this meeting and the following offers an interesting account of the meeting.

THE *EASTBOURNE GAZETTE.* WEDNESDAY, 15 MARCH 1939

WOMEN AND LOCAL AFFAIRS

Hove Councillor's Advice TO MEADS WOMEN CONSERVATIVES

The newly-formed Meads Women's Branch of the Eastbourne Conservative Association held their second meeting at Steivlo Court on Friday. At this meeting the branch was fortunate in having their principal speaker Councillor Miss Kenyon Stow, of Hove, who is an authority on local Government, which formed the subject of her address. The meeting was held in the hall built in memory of the old boys of Warren Hill who fell in the Great War. The room, through the kindness of the present owners, is proving a great asset to Stelvio Court. The open fireplace was filled with coral pink begonias, and begonias also decorated the speaker's table.

Mrs Crompton Peatfield, chairman of the Meads Branch, presided and welcomed fifty-eight members. With her on the platform were Mrs F. Taylor (hon. secretary and treasurer) and Miss Lloyd Jones. Among others present were: Mrs E. Bousfield, Mrs Cogswell, Miss Wilton, Mrs Smith, Miss Royan, Mrs Poole, Mrs MacMillan (head of the tea committee), Mrs Laws. Mrs Knight, Miss Jarvis, Mrs Howey, Miss Gerry, Mrs C. Ford, Mrs Eskroyd, Mrs Dean, Miss Curtis, Mrs Gore Brown and members of the committee, including Mrs Bradford, Mrs Dean, Miss Dalby, Miss Harding, Mrs Perrv, Mrs Scott and Mrs Verrall. The chairman mentioned it had been decided that future meetings would be held on the first Tuesday of each month instead of the first Friday, so as not to clash with other events taking place in the town. There would be one more meeting (on April 4) and a garden meeting during the summer months, when it was hoped their Member, Mr Charles Taylor, would address them. Mrs Swan, who had been co-opted as a member of the committee, could not attend on Friday as she was suffering from Influenza, and Mrs Stevens sent apologies for her absence. Mrs Peatfield, in calling attention to the minimum subscription of one shilling, suggested that those who were able should do more, as the subscriptions included six or seven meetings and the monthly magazine and the desire of the committee was to obtain the very best speakers. Teas were served at the modest charge of two pence each person.

LOCAL GOVERNMENT-MINDED

Councillor Miss Kenyon Stow was introduced as one who knew her subject well. She has been member of the Hove Town Council for twelve years, and the chairman of several committees; and she soon mode it plain to the Meads women that such a position was no sinecure. "You either get absorbed by it and never want to leave or else you become bored and your interest peters out", she said. She advised her hearers to become more "local government-minded" and deplored the apathy which prevailed when only 30 per cent of local women recorded their votes on polling day. She reminded them of the importance of the franchise both in relation to parliamentary and local government affairs.

The administration of various Acts of Parliament, she continued, had increased the work of local authorities enormously, particularly those dealing with public health, child welfare, education and housing. Last century the public health visitor was unknown, but now seven and eight million visits were paid annually by these workers. She was convinced that pubic health services and education should work hand in hand, and she was glad that the social services were not being cut down but were expanding under the present Government.

Interesting details were given of the health and medical services carried on in the schools and clinics at Hove. The question was raised whether the higher rents in some of the new housing areas did not restrict the food supply. Food was more important than houses in the health of the nation and it was feared that many living in those new areas were under-nourished. In conclusion, the speaker spoke out with great warmth of feeling for the Prime Minister, and deplored the criticism that had been levelled at him, not only by the Socialists but by people of their own party, who seemed to forget that he had saved the country when it was on the brink of war. Thanks were expressed to the speaker by Mrs E. Bousfield and Miss Lloyd Jones.

CHAPTER SEVEN

Spiritual and Religious Life

Today on a walk around Eastbourne you will find many examples of places of worship, with St Mary's Church in the Old Town area claiming to have ancient cellars and links to the monks at The Lamb Inn dating back to the eleventh century. In the 1830s, the Trinity Church and Chapel were opened with Christ Church being consecrated in 1864. St Saviour's Church was consecrated in 1867 with St John's Church opening in 1870 to accommodate the growth of people moving to the area who were looking for somewhere to worship. After this period several more churches opened up, including St Andrew's Presbyterian Church in 1878, All Souls Church in 1881, St Anne's Church in 1883, Ceylon Place Baptist Church in 1885, St Peter's Church, designed by Henry Currey, in 1894, to name a few. Many of these still remain today, although numbers of worshippers have declined over the decades.

During the nineteenth century, religion played a huge part in the lives of many families in Victorian England, with Sundays being reserved for attending church or chapel and worship. All activity was serious and solemn with children being asked to be on their best behaviour and be quiet. Although the Church of England was still very popular and drew the crowds, the Nonconformist chapels were beginning to attract a greater number of people as they also organised trips to the seaside, the countryside and arranged events such as lace making and choir classes. They also organised events to raise money for these activities.

Methodism became very popular throughout the country as it had a new energy and was especially popular among industrial workers. The Nonconformist clergy came from all walks of life and were not just limited to the upper classes, as had been the case previously. Many of them were working people or had started off as lay preachers within their communities. The church buildings were usually constructed within the community and paid for by public conscription. The seating plans were open and varied and allowed people to mix, and for them to sit where they felt comfortable in a place of worship. Both Methodist and Baptist ministers were used to playing a role in political movements of the time and many of them would take part in public speaking.

Religion and the church now, regardless of denomination, provided a strong social centre for many people – most churches had numerous activities and clubs attached to them. Inner towns and cities offered theatrical events, dances and balls, while the more rural communities offered more low-key entertainment in the form of groups which were aimed at girls, such as reading groups, girl guide groups, needlework and bible classes.

Spiritual Life

Other women turned to religion to help with the losses they had suffered during the First World War or the uncertainty as to whether or not a husband or son would be seen again. During the 1930s, many new churches were built and one in the Eastbourne area was the church of St Elisabeth on Victoria Drive. This building was commented on in many guide books of the time as being quite remarkable in appearance and was a bold experiment in ecclesiastical architecture and fittings.

Many turned to an alternative approach and turned to spiritualism which has since had a presence in Eastbourne. Whether you believe in the afterlife and spirits is entirely your own choice but many people who have been through struggles in their lives find great comfort from it.

A book about the lives of Eastbourne women cannot be complete without some mention of a few of the spirits which have chosen to live on in this special seaside town. Whether you choose to believe in ghosts or not these few short stories give a glimpse of the history and the hauntings of Eastbourne.

The Redoubt Fortress Ghost

With its hidden secret tunnels dating back over 200 years, the Redoubt Fortress is something of a treasure in Eastbourne. All along the south-east coast were several fortifications built to keep out Napoleon's troops in the early 1800s, which still remain and stand proud today. The redoubt it is the home to a vast collection of fascinating snippets from the past and has many connections with the military history of the area. Here you can discover what Eastbourne was like during the Second World War and what wartime life was like here by the sea. You can also look on in wonder at the many medals awarded to local men for their time spent in the Royal Sussex regiment from when it was formed in 1701.

The Redoubt Fortress, which can be found along the seafront in Eastbourne, is said to be haunted by the ghost of a young lady who met her solider sweetheart here in the mid-1800s. They would meet in secret and often spend nights together in the hidden tunnels so that no one would find them or discover their secret plans to marry. The young lady was from a very well-to-do family and her father had a suitable young gentleman arranged to marry her. However, the young lady did not want to marry a stranger for whom she had no feelings; she wanted to marry her soldier and so they planned to marry once he returned from battle that spring.

However, the young man never returned to her or to Eastbourne and on hearing of her fiancé's death in action, the young lady threw herself from Beachy Head to her death in the waters below.

The young lady's unhappy spirit lingers on today and many people have reported seeing a figure dressed in a very grand style, walking in the redoubt. Many believe that this is her spirit hoping one day she will be reunited with her fiancé so that they will be together for always.

The Devonshire Park Theatre Ghost

Experts in the field of the paranormal believe that there are many different sorts of spirits who choose to haunt places for various reasons, one example of these are orbs. Orbs have long fascinated people and one reason is that no one can say for certain what they are. Whether you think that they are just dust specks which get caught on film or tricks of the light, or – as many ghost hunters like to think – a message from the spirit world, one thing is certain: they fascinate millions. Many people feel great comfort from the appearances which remain unexplained, and there are an increasing number of reports of many orbs of different colours by people and paranormal research groups who investigate the phenomena. It is not just these groups who have experienced orb activity, as this has been reported at the Devonshire Park Theatre over the years by people in the audience and people who have worked at the theatre.

The Devonshire Park Theatre is a fine example of Victorian architecture and was built in 1884 and designed by the same architect as the Winter Garden, Henry Currey. It was named after the Duke of Devonshire, who is the landowner of this area. The reason the theatre was built on this location is because the duke originally prohibited the building of a theatre anywhere on his land as he considered it tawdry and sleazy and not becoming of the gentry he wished to attract to the town. It was thought that these sorts of activities should be kept to the neighbouring towns of Hastings and Brighton. However, due to the popularity of music halls in other, poorer areas of the town, it was realised that there was money to be made and so he allowed his own theatres to be built, the first being the Devonshire Park.

Back in the early days of theatre the colour blue was very expensive to create, and whether it be for lighting, décor or material, it was used very sparingly. Green and yellow were considered unlucky in theatre, as it was said that the devil would disguise himself by wearing a hat or tie in these colours.

The orbs that appear at the Devonshire Park are said to be the spirit of Annabella Charleston who sang at the theatre when it was first opened. She was renowned for her beautiful bright blue dresses, made from the finest quality textiles from exotic lands. It was said that she died of a broken heart when she discovered that her husband was having an affair with another singer. She was found hanging in the theatre dressing room. It is thought that her spirit has chosen to linger on in a place where she was most happy.

All Saints Hospital, Meads

There is a ghost story which relates to the beautiful old hospital which was once in the Meads area of Eastbourne. At the time that the grand building was constructed in 1869, Meads was a very lush and green area of the town. Today little has changed, except that it has become slightly more built up with the rise in population. All Saints existed as a convalescent hospital from 1869 until 1959. The building itself was beautiful and had a gentle and calming feel about it. Throughout the building there were many great examples of stained glass depicting different saints. Although sadly the hospital building is long gone, there is something of yesteryear that lingers on in this part of the town. One lady who used to live in this area told me of the figures she would often see around the same time in the early evening in the old hospital. She described the two figures as females and dressed in an old style of nurse's uniform with the capes and caps, and they always linked arms as they walked quite happily along. They were only ever seen around the same time of an evening and the lady assumed they must have been heading to work for the start of their shift. There was some information found about two nurses from All Saints who had contracted cholera from patients and sadly passed away. The lady who told me this story strongly believed that these two figures were indeed spirits and not of today. However, she said that she never felt afraid – in fact the opposite. The lady moved away so was unable to keep up with her spectral contact and wonders if anyone else has witnessed any similar sighting in the Meads area.

Bibliography

Ashelford, Jane, *National Trust – The Art of Dress 1500–1914*, National Trust, 1996, London

Brown, Tina, *Haunted Theatres of East Sussex*, The History Press, 2005

Eastbourne, Illustrated Guide Books, 1930

Ginn, Peter; Goodman, Ruth and Langlands, Alexander, *The Edwardian Farm*, Pavilion Books, 2010

Ginn, Peter; Goodman, Ruth and Langlands, Alexander, *The Wartime Farm*, Mitchell Beazley, 2012

Grieves, Keith, *Sussex in the First World War*, Sussex Record Society, 2004

Hodges, Peter R., *Temples of Dreams* SB Publications, 1994, Seaford

Pugh, Peter, *The Grand Hotel 1875-2000*, Cambridge Business Publishing, 2000, Sussex

Surtees, J., *Barracks, Workhouse and Hospital*, Eastbourne Local History Society, 1992

The Vintage Fashion Guild, *History of Fashion*, London

Wojtczak Helena, *Women of Victorian Sussex*, Hastings Press, 2003

The National Trust Archives, www.nationaltrust.org.uk

www.sussexhistory.net/2017/08/26/a-first-for-sussex-women

www.womenofeastbourne.co.uk

www.edflhg.uk (East Dean and Friston Family History Group)

www.photohistory-sussex.co.uk

www.britishnewspapersarchive.co.uk

Acknowledgements

I would like to thank Laura Murphy and the lovely ladies of the WayfinderWoman (www.wayfinderwoman.com) for sharing with me some of their amazing research into the Women of Eastbourne over the last two hundred years and also for introducing me to some remarkable women associated with the town whose stories will continue to be heard.

I would also like to thank:

Janet Gadd, Eastbourne

Edward Thomas, Eastbourne

Lloyd Brunt, East Dean and Friston Family History Society

The Grand Hotel, Eastbourne

Index